P9-APN-023

WATERS OF FIRE

WATERS OF FIRE

Sister Vandana

AMITY HOUSE
WARWICK, NEW YORK

Published by Amity House, Inc.
16 High Street
Warwick, New York 10990

© 1988 by Vandana

First published 1981 by The Christian Literature Society, Madras, India

All rights reserved. No part of this publication may be reproduced or transmitted, in any form or by any means, without permission in writing from the publisher.

Cover design by William D. Donovan

ISBN: 0-916349-31-4

Library of Congress Number 87-72987

This book is respectfully dedicated to Swami Chidanandji, whose gracious kindness made it possible for me to live by the Gangaji — to hear her incessant *AUM* and to become one with her flow.

Contents

Introduction   1

Chapter 1   Waters of Recognition, John 1:29-34   7

Chapter 2   Water — God's Extravaganza, John 2:1-11   19

Chapter 3   Waters of Rebirth, John 3:1-5   31

Chapter 4   Living Streams, John 4:14   50

Chapter 5   Healing Waters, John 5:1-15   64

Chapter 6   Walking on the Waters, John 6:16-21   77

Chapter 7   Water to Drink, John 7:37-39   90

Chapter 8   The Guru's Pad-Puja, John 13:1-20   105

Chapter 9   Waters of Salvation, John 19:31-37   122

Chapter 10   Epilogue — Waters of Awakening, John 21:1-23   139

Appendix   I   Waters in the Vedic Tradition   147

Appendix II   The Sacred Ganges   158

Appendix III   Water in *Sandhya-Vandanam*   170

Notes   175

Glossary of Terms   183

Introduction

If any man thirst, let him come to me and drink; and out of his
heart shall flow streams of living water: he who believes in me.
This He said of the Spirit...

John 7:37-38

Water in the Bible, as in the Indian and other traditions, is a symbol
of God's life-giving, purifying, thirst-slaking, sanctifying activity.
Perhaps in no other book of the Bible is water used an an instrument
— a mere "excuse" — (*nimitta matra* as the Gita would say) — of God's
vivifying power. In many chapters of his Gospel the beloved disciple
shows how water has become the means, the occasion or the instrument
of His grace outpoured on man (humanity).* I propose to go through
the relevant chapters of this Gospel, commenting on this aspect of "Sister
Water."

"Be praised, my Lord, through Sister Water, for greatly useful,
lowly, precious, chaste is She," wrote Francis of Assisi in his canticle.
These adjectives describing water are very apt; each of them is seen
in the way water is *used* by John, as we shall see in the course of the
commentary. But, it may be asked, why a *commentary*? why on *St.
John*? and why the theme of *Water*?

* Note: "man" throughout the book stands for humanity.

1

1. Why a commentary?

The first two questions can both be answered by the fact that my study is largely inspired by my interest in Indian theologizing. Reflection and commentaries on the Scriptures — *bhashyas* — are the normal mode used in India for growth in the spiritual life, for that is surely the goal of all theologizing — coming closer to God till we are one with Him. Even today much of the study and meditation in Indian spirituality is done through the various commentaries on the *Shastras* (Scriptures). It is fitting that Christians in India, but also in the West today, should adopt this method more than speculation on dogmas and articles of the faith.

Two centuries of rationalistic historicism have helped to obscure the tradition that the New Testament is first and foremost a collection of theological documents. The Gospels are not biographies of Jesus but interpretations of the message of salvation proclaimed in the words and works of Jesus, the anointed of God.[1] A theological study of these documents in India would necessarily mean a prayerful study; theologizing in a contemplative way, not merely thinking "about" God's words and works but thinking "with" Him, in His Presence, and ultimately being drawn beyond thought and sesne into this very depth. Theologizing would then be an experiential and heart knowledge of God, not merely academic and cerebral. The theologizer must be an experiencer and a meditator.[2] He should strive, while reading the Scriptures, to get the depth meaning (not merely the primary (literal) or secondary implied meaning) — which is experienceable but not expressible. This, I feel, would be equally true of an Eastern or Western theologizer. Today, for both, experiencing God seems more important than knowing about Him.

In the ninth century A.D. in India, there lived Anandavardhana, who first spoke of *akvani* as the soul of poetry — *Kavyasyatma dhvaniritti*. He says the reader should be a *rasajinata* — one who experiences the atmosphere of *rasdhvani* created by the poet whose language is evocative. The reader must have the sensitivity to be able to relish and enjoy the same *rasa* (the juice). As St. Ignatius of Loyola put it: *Non abundantia scientiae sed sentire et gustare res interne* ("Not

an abundance of knowledge but to feel and relish the inner thing.'')
Only such a reader, I feel, would be able fully to enter into the spirit
of John's Gospel and resonate and respond to the intuitions of him who
leaned on Jesus' heart and described its being pierced open on the cross.

This *dhvani* way of reading and commenting on the Scriptures might
be called the approach of the heart. Since the scientific revival of the
sixteenth to seventeenth centuries the interpretation of the Bible has been
done mostly with the head (historical, literary, form criticism, etc.).
A great deal has perhaps been missed out on in this way, in failing to
appreciate that ''the familiar and mundane story of Jesus is the way
through which one arrives at the experience of God,'' whereas rhetorical
or metaphorical criticism can evoke a limited experience of the
Transcendent, so utterly beyond conceptualization. G. Soares-Prabhu
remarked that this insight has unfortunately not been followed up and
that we have hardly any examples of metaphorical or *dhvani* interpretations of non-parabolic New Testament texts and adds, ''A fruitful field
of exploration lies open here.''[3] I found here an invitation and a
challenge.

One recalls Dr. Robin Boyd's saying in ''The Shape of Indian
Christian Theology'' (*The Indian Journal of Theology, January-March
1973*) that Indian theology would do well to express itself by means
of commentary on scriptural texts rather than by a body of systematic
Christian theology along western lines. I found further encouragement
to venture on this study by the positive comments made on a former
attempt of mine: *''A Reflection on an Upanishadic Text in the Light
of the Johannine Gospel — From Death to Life.''*[4]

2. Why St. John?

St. John, rather than any other book in the Bible or another
evangelist, is chosen because his method of presenting Christ-Life is
eminently suited to the Indian psyche and spirit. Several of the reasons
given below apply today equally to the psyche and spirit of the Westerner.
John's Gospel is considered ''spiritual'' and ''mystical'' — as Swami
Abhishiktananda has shown in his writings, in terms of advaitic vision
and mystic experience. This responds to the needs of today's Western

God-seekers, many of whom are interested in Eastern spirituality and
mysticism, which is in several ways akin to John's. Also John has
relevance for modern India, as M.M. Thomas, S.V. Mathew and
Christopher Duraisingh have shown.[5] John's writings, with their own
special stresses and insights, perfectly fulfil the test of a theology —
especially for the East, India in particular.

Perhaps it would also be true to say that on the whole John suits
India's ethos better than Paul, because in him we see theology revolving
around the axis of a Creation-Incarnation-Resurrection — New Creation
Complex, while in Paul the axis is more the Fall-Cross-Redemption-
Judgment Complex.[6] While the latter may have more interest to
Protestant theology, the former would suit Indians — specifically the
Hindu's idea of Creation-Avatar-Realization, and here again today's
trend in the West, too, perhaps. Furthermore, the contrast principles
of truth-untruth, light-darkness, life-death, found in John fit in with
India's desire for "passover" from *Asat* to *Sat* (from unreality to
Reality), from *tamas* to *Jyoti* (from darkness to light), from *mrtyu* to
amrtam (from death to life).[7] In John *Moksha* is not a blessedness and
liberation after death but — as also in Hinduism — a consciousness *(Chit)*
of the Truth *(Sat)* which is bliss *(Anandam)* here and now, born already,
from abiding in His love.

C. Duraisingh, in the "reasons" he gives for the relevance of John
to the world of India today says that Jesus' attitude to worship expressed
in John 4 is "conducive to the evoking of a meaningful theology" (he
adds, "of liturgy amidst true secularity "). Transcendence can never
be localized and no spot on earth — neither "the temple" nor "this
mountain" — can be called holy or profane; for what is important is
the self-transcending relationship to the Father "in spirit and in truth."

This the Hindu would very readily understand and accept, though
perhaps for different reasons from those of the modern protagonist of
secularity, sociality, or social justice. Whether we think of John's Gospel
as more dynamic or more mystical and advaitic; whether his terminology
is more Hebraic and open to the non-Jewish world; whether his "I and
the Father are one" suits the advaitic understanding of union — (which
to the traditional Christian is still rather taboo) — all these are questions that may be debated. But that his cyclic, contemplative, discours-
ing approach has an appeal today and not only to the Indian thinker,
cannot be doubted.

There is yet another reason that John's Gospel and theology would appeal to the Indian mind and heart. In discussing the significance of Johannine Theology, Bruce Vawter says: "The first task in evaluating the significance of any theologian is to isolate his contribution from that of his contemporaries and predecessors, thereby to see both his dependent relationships and his originality."[8] The first element he singles out in John that most strikingly differentiates him from the Synoptics is the transfer of interest from establishment of the Kingdom to the *person of Jesus Himself*. Whether it is an exaggeration to say that this change of emphasis "is the first great departure from primitive Christianity," it is certain that the stress on the Person of Jesus has an appeal to the Indian far more than "the Kingdom." I have seen the latter idea awaken and interest the Hindus when the kingdom of God is mentioned as being *within you*. But the person of Jesus always has had an attraction and elicits unfailing reverence and admiration, even when, like Gandhiji, they reject Christianity but maintain that they love Christ. John emphasized precisely those elements most relevant to the Christianity of his day and put them in a language comprehensible to that age; more than this we can ask no theology to do. In John, as Dodd says, "Whatever influences may have been present have been masterfully controlled by a powerful and independent mind... There is no book, either in the New Testament or outside it, which is really *like* the fourth Gospel."[9] For these reasons, then, I have chosen this Gospel rather than any other book of the Bible, for my special study in this essay at theologizing — through water.

3. Why the theme of water?

This may be due more to a personal reason than to the objective importance of the water-symbolism found in many spiritual traditions. Water has a special and powerful attraction for me. The waters of life flowing from the Temple, from His Heart, slaking the soul who comes to draw at the well, as did the Samaritan woman in chapter four and herself being turned into a "stream of living water" — as so graphically depicted by Jyoti Sahi in his painting — all these find a very meaningful resonance in my God-seeking heart. Then, too, perhaps living for some months each year by the beautiful, gently flowing Gangaji,[10] listen ing to her unceasing *Om* calling, recalling one constantly to "Come to the Father,"[11] may also have much to do with my predilection for water. Anyone who has enjoyed leisure of heart to sit still at the banks of any stream, and perhaps very specially a holy river like the Ganges, will understand why I have chosen this theme.

For this reason, a section on the Ganga in particular and waters in the Vedic tradition in general is added — to make this essay more relevant to a Christian in India or anyone interested in Indian spirituality.

May St. John, who leaned on that Heart of Christ and listened to its heartbeats, help us to drink deep of the life-giving stream of the Spirit that is poured out from that pierced Heart on the world and on "any man who thirsts."

> *OM! Shri Yesu Jeevanjaldayakaya namah!*
> OM! Prostrations to Jesu the giver of living waters!

CHAPTER ONE

Waters of Recognition

John 1:29-34

John the Baptist "appeared at Bethany on the far side of the Jordan" (Jn. 1:28). Thus, straightaway, the herald who came announcing the Messiah introduces us to "Waters."

The waters of Jordan were to be the venue of Jesus' first public appearance in this Gospel. "It was," John said, "to reveal Him to Israel that I came baptizing with water" (Jn. 1:31). He justifies his baptism of water as a preparation for the Messiah and in order to make known "the One you do not Know," who "is already in Israel's midst" (Jn. 1:26-7). The waters here become a means of making known the Saviour.

1. Recognition

Yet the Baptist twice admits that he "did not know who He would be" (Jn. 1:31 and 33), though the express purpose of his baptizing was to prepare men for His coming. Only in the act of baptizing the Messiah in the Jordan waters, the Baptist recognized Him — Him whom "the

world did not recognize" (Jn. 1:15) — for "He who sent me to baptize
with water had said to me: 'You will see the Spirit come down and
stay on a man; he is the One who baptizes with the Holy Spirit"
(v. 33). The waters were thus the first "witness" of the first recognition of Jesus.

Only He on whom the Spirit comes down and rests can baptize in
the Spirit. John had said, "I baptize with water" only. An outpouring
of the Spirit in the Messianic age had been prophesied by the Old Testament prophets. Isaiah had foretold that the Spirit would rest on the
Messiah (11:2); "I have filled Him with my Spirit" (42:1). (Cf. Is.
32:15; 12:3; Joel 2:28 f.; Jer. 2:13; Ezek. 39:29; 47:1 f; Zech. 12:10,
etc.)

No doubt the Baptist would have understood "the Spirit resting
on Him" only in the Old Testament sense, as signifying God's vital
power. Later, the Spirit's coming was recognized as a distinct divine
agent, a teaching much stressed in the second half of John's Gospel.
The Baptist did not have the Christian revelation of the Holy Spirit as
a distinct person in the Godhead.[1]

2. Water — symbol of the Spirit

Later in John's Gospel, living water comes to be (as we shall see)
the very symbol of the Spirit Himself (cf. Jn. 7:37-9). In the Old Testament, water, especially spring water, had symbolized the life that God
gave, particularly in the Messianic age. In the New Testament, too,
the Lamb, the Shepherd, were to lead them to "the springs of living
water" — pointing to Eschatological waters (cf. Rev. 7:17). All who
want this Life and "thirst for it" would have "the water of life and
have it free" (Rev. 22:17). In the same verse, too, the Spirit — invariably
linked to water — is also mentioned: "The Spirit and the Bride say,
'Come'. . . Then let all who are thirsty, come."

3. A marriage

A marriage between water and the Spirit seems, then, to have taken
place from the very first chapter of Genesis — even before light was

created. We are told, "The raging ocean that covered everything was engulfed in total darkness and the power of God (the Spirit of God) was moving over the Water" (Gen. 1:2, Good News Bible translation) or, as the Jerusalem Bible translation puts it: "Now the earth was a formless void, there was darkness over the deep, and God's Spirit hovered over the water." The "hovering" reminds one of Deuteronomy 32:11: "Like a bird hanging in the air over its young in the nest." "Like a bird!" — at the Baptism of Jesus, too, the Spirit appeared as a dove. In the flood at the time of Noah, the dove, bearing an olive branch in its beak, foreshadowed the fragrance of Christ; but here it is the Holy Spirit coming in the form of a dove "who shows that the Lord is merciful."[2] The Spirit is gentle — like a mother's love. Has it not been called the feminine aspect or element in the Trinity and has it not been depicted as a woman in the art of the Orthodox Church? Might it not be, equally correctly, called the *Shakti* of God, the power of God that moved, hovered, not over the formless void, but over the waters? In other places, too, in the Old Testament, as well as the New, the Spirit and water are linked together. "I shall pour clean water over you; . . . I shall put my Spirit into you" (Ezek. 36:27). Peter at Pentecost would attribute the miracle his hearers had witnessed, to the "pouring out of the spirit" by the Risen Christ (Acts 2). The very expression *poured* suggests water — though actually the Pentecostal Spirit appeared as "tongues of fire."

In the Vedic tradition, too, fire and water are often linked; fire *agni* is born of water. In the hymn *"Apo Devih"* (Rig Ved. VII 49:6) we read:

> Within the waters, Soma has told me remedies exist of every sort
> and Agni, who brings blessings to all.

St. Proclus, Bishop of Constantinople, cries out, "Come, see these new and stupendous wonders: I mean the sun of justice bathing in the Jordan fire immersed in water, and God sanctified by the intermediary of men."[3] The Spirit is both *fons vivus* and *ignis caritas* as we pray in the *"Veni Creator Spiritus"*.

"I proclaim with the voice of a herald," cries Pseudo-Hippolytus in his sermon on the Epiphany. "Come, all tribes of nations . . . This is the water which partakes of the Spirit, it waters paradise, it causes the earth to drink, it makes the plant to grow; in a word, it regenerates man by causing him to be reborn. . . In that water the Son came to wash man in the water and Spirit. . . I want to go back to the fountain of life and to cause the stream of all remedies to break forth."[4]

It is when man abandons God — "the fountain of living waters" — for his own "leaky cisterns" of sin (cf. Jer. 2:13) that the fires of purification are needed. Cleansing and purification become a necessity. The Baptist came "proclaiming a baptism of repentance for the forgiveness of sins" (Mk. 1:4; Lk. 3:4). Thus the baptismal waters are also purifying waters.

Paul, again linking water and the Spirit, says to Titus: "God saved us. . . by means of the cleansing waters of rebirth and by renewing us with the Holy Spirit" (Tit. 3:5).

4. Purifying waters

The bath of regeneration and renewal in the Holy Spirit are bracketed together, the reference no doubt being to Christian baptism, as in Eph. 5:2-6 where the same term is used — *Loutran* (bath). He made the church clean by washing her in water so that she would be glorious, with no speck or wrinkles but holy and faultless. It is a bath of regeneration. The symbolism of water finds its complete meaning in Christian baptism.[5] John used the waters of Jordan which had formerly cleansed Naaman the Leper (2 Kings 5:10-14). But baptism is here seen to bring about primarily not the cleansing of the body but "of the conscience" (1 Pet. 3:21). It is a bath that cleanses us from our sin through the outpouring of the Spirit who is "the remission of sin."

In the Hindu tradition, too, it is always through the waters that man feels he is purified: "May the waters, the mothers, purify us" (Tait. Samhita 1.21) and again, "Hail to you, divine, unfathomable, all-purifying waters!" (T.TS. 1.2.3) In the Rig Vedic hymn (vii. 49) to the divine waters, one almost sees a prefiguring of the Lord Jesus in the waters:

> In the midst of the waters is moving the Lord surveying men's truths and men's lies. How sweet are the waters, crystal clear and cleansing! Now may these great, divine waters quicken me! (v 3)

"Quickening" means life-giving. Is not Jesus at his baptism the true Varuna, who could "survey all men's truths and lies" and "quicken" them to the true life?

> From whom King Varuna, Soma and all the deities drank exhilarating strength, Into whom the universal Lord has entered. Now may these great, divine waters quicken me! (v. 4)

and verse 8 sings:

> Whatever sin is found in me
> Whatever wrong I may have done
> I have lied or falsely sworn
> Waters, remove it far from me.

As Christians believe that in the baptismal waters, by the power of the Spirit, all sins, no matter how heinous, are wiped away and that they are "quickened," brought to a participation in the new life — the life of the Triune God, so Hindus believe that all their sins are washed away in the Ganges if they bathe with faith and devotion. For the origin of the Ganga is ascribed to God Himself. St. John's baptism, too, was one of "repentance for the forgiveness of sins" (Matt. 1:14, Lk. 3:3). The Synoptics show that repentance was sought not simply for personal sins "but in the manner of great prophets of Israel, for sins of national failure, to fulfill the responsibilities properly to be discharged by a true people of God."[6]

5. Inner purification by the Spirit of Christ

Christ standing in the Jordan waters might be taken as a sign and fulfillment of all the washings, bathings, purifications — for the sins of all men, of all times. However, as in India and anywhere on earth where frail man lives, so, too, in the Old Testament the ritual washings with water (doubtless of Semitic origin, enumerated in priestly legislation) became more and more prominent in later Judaism, until the washings became an end in themselves, losing their inner spiritual and liturgical meaning — as can happen even today in religious practices and ceremonials of all religions. That is why one has constantly to come back to the reminder of Jesus about worship of "the Father in spirit and in truth" (Jn. 4:23) and his vehement words to the Pharisees who condemned His disciples for eating with unclean hands." "It is the things that come out of a man that make him unclean for it is from within, from men's hearts, that evil intentions emerge; fornication, theft, murder, adultery, avarice, malice, deceit, indecency, envy, slander, pride, folly. All these things come from within and make a man unclean" (Mk. 7:21-23). No amount of bathing, immersions, washings in the purest of waters can cleanse man, unless he be reborn of the Spirit; the Spirit that moved over, and ever moves over waters, unless God says to him again, as he did in Ezekiel 36:25, "I shall pour clean waters over you and you will be cleansed. I shall cleanse you of all your defilement and of all your idols. I will give you a new heart and put a new spirit into you. I shall remove the heart of stone from your bodies and give you a heart of flesh instead. I shall put my spirit in you and make you keep my laws..."

6. Justification by the Spirit of the Risen Lord

The effusion of the Spirit, as the Baptist stated, will be effected through the Messiah, but He has to be the first recipient of the Spirit, to be able to accomplish his saving work. St. Thomas tells us: "the personal grace whereby the soul of Christ is justified is esssentially the same as his grace by which He is Head of the Church and justifies others" (Summa 3.8.5). But He can confer this Spirit of Justification on others only after His Resurrection. "For Jesus came in corruptible flesh" (Jn. 1:14) and, it is only after He is "lifted up" and at the side of the Father that His body is glorified and fully endowed with life-giving power. Only from then on, the Spirit flows freely from this body as from an inexhaustible spring (Jn. 7:37-9; 19:34; Rom. 5:5). Yet, as is common with St. John, already the radiance of the Father's glory, of whom Jesus is the image, is allowed to peep out, as it were, for men's eyes to look forward to and get accustomed to their eternal gazing. John refers to the fact that "the Spirit, at that time," had not yet been given, because Jesus had not been raised to glory (Jn. 7:39).

7. The baptism of John and of Jesus

Through the rite of baptism or immersion was no innovation (the sectaries of Qumran had made various kinds of ritual washings into an elaborate system), yet John's baptism was different. It was not a self-baptism but was conferred by another. It was a single, unrepeatable act of initiation. It was more like the ritual bath which converts to Judaism had to take before they could be admitted into the holy people, as a sign that they were purified from the "uncleanness" of heathen ways. But baptism in water, he insisted, was only preparatory. The coming One would "Baptize with Spirit and Fire" — a strongly emotive phrase!

However, at Jesus' baptism something happened which altered the current of His life. All four Gospels offer some description, heavily weighted with symbolism. We are entitled to infer that this was the moment at which Jesus accepted His vocation. For Him, and not only for those who wrote about Him, it was the act of God by which He was "anointed for His mission."[7] The Jordan waters were not "waters of recognition" only for John, but also and especially for Jesus. Furthermore, might not one say in terms of Indian and especially Vedantic thought, that they were, for Christ, "waters of Awakening," the moment when He awoke, as it were, to His true "Self," the *Atman*?

8. Waters of awakening

This was surely a moment of fulfillment of the text in Katha Upanishad 3.14 as addressed to the "True Man," the Purush of the Aitareya Upanishad: *Uttishtha Purush...*

"Arise, O man! Arise, awake! You who have received the boons; keep awake." This is, interestingly enough, what the new *sannyasi*, as he plunges into the water, hears from his guru. Then both of them face the rising sun and sing the song to the *Purusha* from *Uttara-Narayana: "Vedahametam Purusham Mahantam..."*

I know Him, that supreme Purusha, sun-colored, beyond all

darkness; only in knowing Him one overcomes death; no other
way exists.

(V. Semhita 31.18)

The Christos, the True Man Himself in this moment is the
Mrtyunjaya, the Conqueror of Death, as One who could say: "I am
the Resurrection and the Life" (JJn. 11:25) and "I am the Way...
No man can come to the Father but by Me" (Jn. 14:6). "No other way
exists!"

Anyone who has intelligently witnessed *Sannyas-diksha* — the
initiation ceremony — by the banks of the Gangaji or any sacred river,
will know and understand something of the real, inner meaning of the
Baptism of Our Lord.

This point of awakening to His Self in the incident, or, rather event
of the Baptism of Christ, is for me the most important and significant.
It is worth pondering on, and, if these reflections are to be of any worth,
they should not remain mere *mananam* (thinking of the Word), but should
pass into *nididhyasanam* (a pondering, lovingly, wordlessly,
thoughtlessly) — in the center of the heart. For that is where this mystery
leads us — "into the secret place of the heart," the *guha*, where alone
the illumination, the awakening to the Self, can take place.

9. *Tat-tvam-asi — Aham Brahmasmi*

When Christ heard the Father's voice saying, "Thou art my Beloved
Son,"[8] it was the Semitic equivalent of the Guru's words to his disciple:
That-tvam-asi, "That thou art," the *Upadesha-mantra* of the Chandogya
Upanishad (6.8.7). And like the disciple who had known now his deepest
self, He answered in His Heart, *"Abba"* — (the Aramaic for "Father,"
to be said only to one from whom one is actually born) — the equivalent
of *Aham Brahmasmi*, the fundamental *mahavakya* of the Brihadaranyaka
Upanishad (1.4.10).

And with this response in His Heart, Jesus "knew" Himself, awoke
as it were, to being the *"Chit" of Saccidananda* — the Hindu "mystery"
nearest to the Trinity — of the being — Consciousness — Bliss. If with
"Thou art my Beloved Son," the Father opened His heart to man, the

Son of Man as "Son" will open His heart and pour out on man, the Spirit — who here appeared as the dove. The appearance of the Spirit, the voice of the Father, the manifestation of the Son standing in the waters — like the High priest uniting in marriage the waters and the Spirit of the Father — here is the first manifestation of the Triune God.

The Father is the *Aham Asmi* — the same "I Am" as Moses had heard on Mount Horeb (Exod. 3:14) as taken in the Greek translation. Deep in his heart the Rishi of India had also heard the same "I Am" as Moses, and loved to meditate on the mystery of Being — *Sat*. We read in Brihadaranyaka Upanishad 1.4.11 and 10:

> In the beginning He said I Am . Thence arose the name I [*aham*].
> He knew himself. He said: I am Brahman.
>
> *Aham Brahmasmi*

In that knowing or consciousness was the thought or *Chit* of the Son. This self-awareness was but the reflection, the mirror, the echo of the unique "I Am," the very name of Yahweh. This ineffable name can only be perceived in the inmost depth of the heart. It is, as Katha Upanishad 1.2.12 puts it:

> not easily perceived, seated deep within, in the abyss, the most
> secret place, primordial.

And it will be from this deepest abyss of His Sacred Heart that later the Son will pour forth His Spirit from the cross — with blood and again with water — on the parched earth of man's heart (Jn. 19:34-7).

10. Logos-*Om-Chit*

This self-awareness or the thought of God in Jesus — the *Chit* — was known to the Greeks as *Logos*. In India, its nearest equivalent is *OM*. When the new Sannyasi emerges from his immersion, the Guru's last brief instruction is to remind him to remain in the consciousness of this inner mystery and so of his total freedom towards all beings —

the mystery of the *advaita*, of the nondual *Brahman;* "while his mind remains totally absorbed in repeating endlessly the sacred *OM* with every breath he takes and every beat of his heart."[9] Jesus is the *OM*, the Logos. In the Johannine theology of the Logos, the functions of the Old Testament hypostatized; dynamic attributes of the *Dabar* Yahweh are eminently verified in the person of Jesus Christ. Christ's "revelatory function" is John's most central theme, by reason of what He is [the Son, the *Chit*, the Word]. He is the Revealer — the manifestation of God; "visible *Patris filius*" as St. Iranaeus put it.[10] Not only is He Son of God: He is the Self-consciousness of God, if one may so put it. He is thus ONE with the Father, "not two," because He is God's very "Consciousness."

11. *Advaita* of Christ — in the Christian Experience

Many theologians like Buber fear to reduce this relationship of the "I" to the self. But as Dupuis rightly points out, theology, while making distinctions which may be partly necessary or useful, has often contributed to neutralize Christian claims. Thus the Christian claim to sonship of God is reduced to a legal fiction if it is reduced to "purely adoption" and "the share in Jesus' own sonship of the Father being lost, there remains no point of entry for *advaita* into the Christian experience."[11] He points out, too, that the Christian experience of God specifically consists of sharing in Jesus' own religious consciousness, that is, in his awareness of divine sonship (cf. Rom. 8:15; Gal. 4:6) and that while the distinction between Jesus and the Father "is an irreducible compound of Jesus' experience," *advaita* has a place in the Christian experience as in that of Jesus Himself: "The Christian shares in Jesus' awareness of his *advaita* with the Father. This is *Christian advaita*."[12]

At the Baptism of Jesus, one was given an inkling of this: "The point of entry" was first revealed to us — viz. the Holy Spirit — the *Atman*. For it is of His Self — the *Atman, the Spirit* — (who appeared over the waters in the form of a dove) — that the Son is conscious, for the Spirit is the *advaita* — the Oneness of the Father and Son. The Spirit, known as *ruah* to the Hebrews, as *pneuma* to the Greeks, refers

to the Inmost Spirit, the source of life within, It would be understood
as "the most intimate core of the conscious being at the level beyond
the reach of sense or mind" — as meaning his *atman*, his self . . . since
he is the deepest center, the very "inwardness" of the divine mystery.[13]
He is the *Antaryami*, the Indweller. When one reaches thus, it is bliss
for He is Bliss, *Anandam*. "This Atman is Brahman" (Brihad Up. 3.4.4)
as Vedic wisdom discovered and teaches. "Know Him as this one Atman
and abandon all discourse."

12. To Bear "the Burden of Christ-Consciousness"

For not in much thinking, speaking, sharing is this bliss to be found,
in being aware only of Him, of this mystery of Saccidananda within,
learning to remain conscious, awakened. But this is a life's work, the
result of intense *sadhana*. It means to be willing to remain silent, hidden
— as Jesus was, for long years before His baptism — to be willing to
enter into "the womb of the waters." How true it is what Sebastian
Moore wrote: "Christians for the most part are distracted. They cannot
bear all the time the burden of Christ-consciousness."[14] Christians, at
least of the West, have begun to suspect and to learn that to bear this
precious burden, to become and to remain aware or conscious of this
Presence of the triune God, they have much to learn from our Buddhist
and Hindu brothers — the way of mindfulness from the former, the
way of yogic meditation from the latter. Both lead to the same end of
bliss whether through the way of nothingness — *sunya* or through the
way of fullness — *purnam*. This was the way, too, which Christ came
to teach: "Let him deny himself — he who wants to follow Me"
(Luke 9:23). For to deny the self is the only way to awaken the Self.

13. From the death of unawareness to the life of Consciousness

For this reason Christ standing in the Jordan — is the *Sannyasi
par excellence* who practiced perfectly before He preached, total renunciation of self. For true *sanyas* is not renunciation of mere possessions,

family status, but rather any *loka* whatever[15], especially of one's "self."
The moment of Christ standing in the waters of His baptism was then
truly his *diksha*, his awakening to the Self. Abhishiktananda writes:
"The awakening [*prabodha*] of Jesus by the Jordan marked his whole
life and consciousness, all his words and actions. This above all is what
he means to share with his disciples in their baptism (immersion) in
Spirit and in Fire.[16] Standing in the waters — between heaven and earth
— He is the bridge, the *pons* — as well at the Pontiff who leads his
people from the death of unawareness and sleep to the life of
consciousness and bliss of His Father, by "passing over" from the self
[the *ahamkar*] — which, as the Baptist so well understood, "must
decrease" — to the Self, which "must increase," until such time as
only He Is! Christ thus answers the agelong Upanishadic prayer:
Mirityorma amritam gamaya, From death lead me to life. (Brihad
Up. 1.3.28)

CHAPTER TWO

Water — God's Extravaganza

John 2:1-11

If it was in the waters of Jordan that Jesus chose to begin His public ministry by humbly going with publicans and sinners to be baptized, it was again through water that he performed the first of his "signs." It is one of the most charming stories in the life of Jesus. Mary, Jesus, and His disciples were invited to a wedding in Cana of Galilee. When wine — used liberally on merry-making occasions — gave out, it was Mary's presence that saved the situation. She turned to Jesus instinctively for help with the certainty of a true *bhakta* (a lover of God). When He seemed to refuse to do anything about it, with equal certainty and the equanimity of a *sthitaprajna* (one of steadfast wisdom)[1], she told the servants just to obey Him. It was at this crucial point that Jesus used His "creature" — water. He told them to fill six large water pots with water and they filled them to the brim. It was the best wine they had ever tasted. Thus through this miracle of water, He revealed His glory and His disciples believed in Him.

1. Water used to manifest His glory

Water! An ordinary, everyday, familiar thing, usually taken for granted and unnoticed — except when found absent and needed. This the Lord used as an instrument to "manifest His glory," or "He let His glory be seen" through it, "and His disciples believed in Him" (Jn. 2:11, Jerusalem Bible translation). God often uses very ordinary things and lets His glory shine out through them. One is tempted perhaps to call water God's favorite creation! It may be worthwhile, then, to look at water in His first creation and then in St. John's Gospel — as an aid to understanding better the miracle of Cana in Galilee.

2. Water in Genesis and St. John

It is interesting to note that in the first half of John's Gospel, called "the Book of Signs," the seven-day structure of the original creation story is imitated, culminating in this first manifestation of Jesus' glory.[2]

Three days later there was a wedding at Cana in Galilee (2:1), i.e., that is, three days after the meeting of Jesus with Philip and Nathaniel. The opening events of the Gospel, therefore, are contained within one week, of which almost every day is noticed.[3] That John 2:1 introduces an event that occurs on "the third day" doubtless has yet another symbolism. But for our purpose, it is interesting to see how water is treated in the original creation story.

Water appears first in Genesis 1:2 as "the raging ocean covering everything engulfed in darkness and the power of God moving over the waters on the first day. On the second day God said, "Let there be a dome to divide the water" (Gen. 1:6). On the third day God commanded , "Let the water below the sky come together in one place, so that the land will appear... and He named the water sea" (Gen. 1:9-10). God had not yet finished with water. He said, "Let the water be filled with many kinds of living beings... He blessed all and told the creatures that live in the water to reproduce, and to fill the sea... Evening passed and morning came — that was the fifth day (Gen.

1:20-23). Thus on four out of the six days of creation, God dealt with water. "From the waters is this universe produced." No wonder we read this in the Vedas in the Satpatha Brahmana VI.8.2.4.

St. John, while apparently alluding to the seven-day structure of the original creation story, shows the same predilection for water as God does — the way he uses it in a variety of circumstances throughout his narrative of Jesus' life — now as a "venue" for His appearance, now for healing, now as a symbol of His life, now as a lesson in humility, now as signifying the pouring out of His Spirit. Here, in this His first miracle, Jesus used water as an instrument of his first "sign."

3. "This was the first of the signs given by Jesus" (Jn. 2:11)

In Israel, as in India, miracles and wonders were often looked for in prophets and saints, and were considered a seal of God on such men. There are many wonder-working "Sai Babas" found in the Old Testament.

In fact, the term *signs* comes from the Old Testament background in which it especially meant Yahweh's wonderful works in the Exodus story (Num. 14:11) "However, what was meaningful about these wonderful deeds was not precisely that they were byond natural causality, but that they had been worked by the God of Israel to reveal Himself to His people. The "signs" of Jesus have exactly this meaning for John and only certain miracles are called "signs."[4] The signs of Jesus constitute the miracles that reveal the nature of Jesus as the revelation of God: these are signs in the Johannine sense.[5] In transforming the waters into wine, this "creative miracle" allowed us to see Jesus as the manifestation of God: "we saw His glory . . . full of grace and truth" (Jn. 1:14).

4. "And the mother of Jesus was there" (Jn. 2:2)

If water were an instrument Jesus used, He also used Mary. When He first manifested His glory, Mary was present, as she was there again at His death on the cross (Jn. 19:25-7). Both these descriptions in John

2 and 19 have several details in common, no doubt on purpose. And in both these events, together with Mary, water was present.

Mary and water have much in common. Mary, like water, was creature — ordinary, unnoticed, quiet, serviceable, lovely, and precious. As there can be no life without water, so God ordained that there would be no new life without Mary. In John, Mary is seen not only in her historical character but in her function in salvation history. The woman of the first creation was called "Life" (Eve) because she was "mother of all the living" (Gen. 3:20). Mary "the woman" — as she will be called again at the foot of the cross — is mother of the new life; not only mother of the Word made flesh, but of all who live by His life. She is the figure of the Church — "the New Eve."[6] And although Jesus said his hour had not yet come, because of her intercession, he anticipates it and her petition is granted. Who can refuse a mother? And Mary is essentially mother.

In all ages and cultures people have sought God in a mother figure. Without making too facile connections, it is interesting to study similarities. Thus in the Vedas the waters are called "mothers." "May the waters, the mothers, purify us!" The Lord is the Son of the waters, born of the waters. "In the waters, Lord, is your seat" (Narayan, Taittiriya Samhita 1.2.2, S.B. VII 4.1.6). Both a mother and a river are venerated with special love in India. The Ganges — the most sacred of all rivers — is always *Gangamata*. When crossing her, pilgrims in the ferries cry out, *"Gangamaya-ki-jai"*. *Arati* is done to her singing:

Om jaya Gange-mata Ekhi Bar jto teri Sharangati ata, Yamkir tras mitakar paramgati pata.

Hail to the Mother Ganges, He who comes to take refuge in you even once will cross the difficulties of death, and find the supreme heaven.

Ganga is called the "refuge" of the *patita* — the fallen ones — as Mary is called "Refuge of sinners," for did not the Lord, dispeller of all sins, dwell in her? There is a story of the Goddess Ganga appearing before King Bhagiratha (who did austere penances to propitiate her) and saying, "All the sinners of the world come to wash away their sins and purify themselves by immersing their sinful bodies in my holy waters. Where shall I wash the immense store of sins they deposit in my watery body?'' Bhagiratha replied: ''O sacred mother, holy saints will bathe in the Ganges and will purge all sins away, for the Lord Vishnu (the all-pervading one), dispeller of all sins, dwells in their heart.'' If Mary is, as we have seen, ''the mother of the new life,'' Gangaji is called ''the nectar of immortality that gives us salvation.'' Over the radio recently I heard a song: *''Hamari zindagi, hamari roti, Gangajike dwara''* (''we receive life and bread through the Ganges''). She it is who gives to us life and bread, and Mary gives to us Jesus, who called Himself our ''Life'' and ''the true Bread of life.'' Some of the prayers addressed to the waters of the Ganga are reminiscent of prayers to the Virgin Mother:

> ''Who can describe,[7] O Mother, thy glory and splendor? O, all powerful Mother of compassion and love!''

Mary and water have yet something else in common. Waters of a river can be very silent, gentle, sometimes as still as a pool; they hardly seem to move, even though the river never ceases to flow from its Source. They can be considerate, cautious as they pass by a rough rock. They are ever ready to give of themselves, to bathe or slake thirst, without ever objecting that too much is asked of them, without expecting a word of gratitude. They are a real example of *Nishkarma karma* that the Gita teaches; service without looking for any reward. They give what they have to give to those who ask or need their help, then pass on, silently, unnoticed, as unspectacularly as they came.

Mary was like that at the wedding feast in Cana — gentle, unobtrusive, quiet, yet able to secure a miracle from a seemingly reluctant Son, with apparent ease through her softly spoken words and her unfailing trust. Lao-tse has said, ''The softest substance of the world goes through the hardest; softness and gentleness are the companions of life. There is nothing weaker than water, but none is superior to it in overcoming the hard, for which there is no substitute. Weakness overcomes strength and gentleness overcomes rigidity.''

Mary, like the waters, and like Dakshinamoorthy in Shankaracharya's Hymn, taught by her *maun vyakhya* (silent discourse). She noticed the need and embarrassment of the wedding party, as the wine came to an end. No one had asked her help, yet she went to her

Son and said gently, "They have no wine" (Jn. 2:3). Jesus answered, "Woman" — which word in the vocative shows no disrespect, as many examples show (e.g., John 19:26) — "You must not tell me what to do" (Good News Bible translation); "You have no claims upon me yet" or "my hours is not yet come" — his hour being his death and exaltation (Jn. 7:30; 8:20; 12:23, 27; 13:1). "What have I to do with you?" seems to draw a line between Mother and Son, especially as the words remind us of those used by demons to Jesus (Mk. 1:24, 5:7, Matt. 8:29). "You have no business with us yet." But Jesus, as always, makes decisions only depending on His Father's will (cf. 11:6). He had refused, too, to act on his brothers' advice and instructions (Jn. 7:6).

Without being deterred by the apparent rebuff, Mary told the servants what to do — in the words of John 2:5: "Do whatever He tells you," — and slipped back into anonymity. She who had spent years listening to His word and pondering it in her heart knew the value of obedience. *Obaudiro:* from listening comes obedience. This had made her know her Son and be sure of His unfailing love. She advised them simply to obey. She knew He would always do what was good, or rather, best.

And "when the steward tasted the water" it was wine. Not only that, but in great abundance and the best they had! Each stone jar, we are told, could hold twenty to thirty gallons (Jn. 2:6).

5. "They filled them to the brim"

Though we are not told — as we are in the miracle of the loaves — how much wine was "left over," we may be sure there was some. Jesus, who could not refuse his mother, had told the servants, "Fill the jars with water" — an apparently crazy thing to say and expect them to do. But they did and "they filled them to the brim" (Jn. 2:7). To the brim! Here we see the extravagance of water — and of love. God does nothing by half measures. Is Jesus not Himself the *pleroma* of God, the plentitude, the *Poornam*? "In Him dwells the fullness of God corporeally." (cf. Col. 2:9; 1:19).

It is interesting that Schoonenberg bases his christology of the enhypostasis of the Word in the man Jesus, and of God's full presence in his human person, on these Pauline texts. Might one not say that Jesus, who was "filled to the brim" with divinity, now sees the servants fill the stone pots "to the brim," so that through this very human act of being present at a wedding and of sensitively saving an embarrassing situation, he could show forth the divinity, with which he was filled, to the full? One begins to see a new meaning — or a new interpretation — in the *Shanti* Path of the Isa Upanishad.

> *Poornamadah, Poornam idam*
> Fullness there (beyond); fullness here.

That is, the fully divine (there) is fully human (here). Christ, who is God's eternal Son, is seen by some modern theologians (like Schoonenberg) as being "threatened to become dehumanized; the man in him risks being undermined to the benefit of the divine person" (*The Christ*, pp. 178-79). John, in this miracle, however, shows Christ to be truly and utterly human, as we have seen. God in Himself as God-made-man walking the earth, is seen living Himself fully — to the full. "Of His fullness we have all received grace upon grace" (Jn. 1:16). The torrents of His grace flow freely on man — without "let or stay," for God is generosity, and what better symbolism is there for this gracious and superabundant giving than waters released in abundance?

All through the Old Testament waters appear "now real, now symbolic, now gentle and life-giving, now destructive and terrifying, now a trickle, now a torrent." In Cana we see it as a torrent — freely given and flowing over. Water in the Bible is always freely given — fronm the first book to the last. In Genesis we read: "When all was *Tohu-tohu* (a mess) — waters were created and flowed freely. On the fifth day God said, "Let the waters abound with life" and in Revelation we read, "Let him receive the water of life freely — who thirsts — come!" The Garden of Eden had to abound in water. "The desert mind, thirsting for beauty, must be told that there was water to make it a paradise, a couple of trees and the four-branched river. Even when sin becomes prevalent, waters are still abundant, and the floodgates of heaven are opened, but now to punish man.[7] Whether it is well water — or the rains sent by Yahweh — it is always in abundance — to show the greatness of His love. The floodwater covered the enemies of Israel as they tried to cross the Red Sea, until they sank into the depths like a stone: "Horse and chariot He cast into the sea" (Exod. 15:1; 5). When Moses struck the rock, waters gushed forth in abundance — a figure, too, of the waters that would gush forth from the side of Christ and become "waters of salvation," which Isaiah foretold we would draw with joy from the Saviour's fountains (Is. 12:3).

The same superabundance is seen in the Gospels and in this miracle of Christ. For if Christ is the infinite self-expenditure of God,[8] was He not Himself to be "poured out like water" for our sake?

Ratzinger, speaking of an "excess" of seven baskets mentioned in Mark 8:8, says:

One thinks at once of a related miracle preserved in the Johannine tradition; the changing of water into wine at the marriage feast at Cana. It is true that the word *excess* does not occur here, but the fact certainly does: according to the evidence of the Gospel, the new-made wine amounted to between 130 and 190 gallons, a somewhat unusual quantity for a private banquet![9] In the Evangelist's view both stories have to do with the central element in Christian worship, the Eucharist. They show it as the divine excess or abundance, which infinitely surpasses all needs and legitimate demands. In this way both stories are concerned, through their reference to the Eucharist,[10] with Christ Himself. And both point back to the law governing the structure of creation, in which life squanders a million seeds in order to save one living one, in which a whole universe is squandered in order to prepare at one point, a place for spirit, for man. Excess is God's trademark in his creation; as the fathers put it: 'God does not reckon his gifts by the measure.' At the same time excess is also the real foundation and form of the history of salvation, which in the last analysis is nothing other than the truly breath-taking fact that God, in an incredible outpouring of himself, expends not only a universe, but his own self, in order to lead man, a speck of dust, to salvation. So excess or superfluity — let us repeat — is the real difinition or mark of the history of salvation. The purely calculating mind will always find it absurd that for man, God himself would be expended. Only the lover can understand the folly of a love to which prodigality is a law, and excess alone is sufficient.[11]

6. "There were six stone water jars standing there" (Jn. 2:6)

Stone was used because, according to Jewish belief, it would not contract ritual uncleanness, just as the Hindu Dharmashastra lays down which materials are considered pure and which not. The Jewish ritual provided for numerous purificaitons by water — as does the Hindu ritual. Hence the water jars were for ablutions customary among the Jews. But all these purifications were powerless to bring about effectively true purity of soul until the New Covenant. Hence Jesus' changing of water into wine is symbolic. At this wedding He foretells it when He changes water (destined for symbolic cleansing) into wine, which symbolizes both spirt (Jn. 15:3) and the purifying word (Jn. 13:10). John sees this changing of water into wine as the replacement of the weak elements of Old Covenant by the rich wine of the New Covenant and Messianic Banquet.[12] It is interesting, too, that Jesus says that His word and teaching will henceforth purify — (rather than ritual washings) in the context of the vine (Jn. 15). The vine being "pruned" means again purification. "You are pruned already by means of the Word I have spoken to you (Jn. 15:3). To be truly purified by God does not mean mere external washings laid down by rituals, but rather to enter into His word and teaching that leads to self-emptying and death. At the washing of the feet of His disciples, Jesus made this clear, though Peter took some time to understand that by refusing to let Jesus wash his feet, he "would have no part" with Him; he would cut himself off from our Lord's ministry and glory if he did not share His outlook and accept the total mystery of self-emptying — even unto love and service of his betrayers.[13]

The water pots at the wedding in Cana remind one, too, of the Indian custom of water pots being piled up at the door of the house where the wedding takes place. Pots with water, as with rice, earth, etc. are symbols of a new life — the *poorna kumbha* — the full pot — filled to the brim — being a symbol of the fullness of life and joy. Laxmi, the Goddess of prosperity, often carries it in one of her four arms.

7. The wine

The wine, too, is symbolic — of joy, celebration, life, love, a new creation, whether as Dodd thinks, the story of the Cana wedding developed out of a parable, or whether, as F.E. Williams thinks, it was based on Luke 5:33-9, together with the tradition of Jesus' mother and brothers. In any case, says Barrett, it seems clear that "John meant to show the supersession of Judaism in the glory of Jesus."[14] It is possible that in so doing he drew material from Dionysiac sources. "There was an exact precedent for the benefaction of Jesus in a pagan worship, doubtless known to some, at least, of John's readers. The god Dionysius was not only the discoverer of wine, but also the cause of miraculous transformation of water into wine (cf. Euripides: Bacchae 704-7, etc.).[15]

So, too, in Vedic India, *Soma* — originally a plant — was raised to the status of a God. The juice of this plant was offered three times a day in a sacrifice — as wine is offered in the Eucharistic sacrifice. If at Pentecost, the apostles, inebriated with the Divine Spirit, were suspected of having drunk too much wine, the gods were often thought to have been inspired by Soma. Thus Indra, for instance, did great and extraordinary deeds. Believed to have grown on the Mujavat mountain, Parjnya, the rain god is, interestingly enough, said to be Soma's father and the waters are his sisters.[16] We find Soma destroying towns, begetting gods, upholding the sky, prolonging mortals' lives. He is also the Lord of the tidal floods.[17] He is given all the attributes given to Indra.[18] For a Christian, wine, transformed into the Blood of Christ at a Eucharistic sacrifice, is believed to give immortality (life everlasting). He would find it interesting to read, in a Rig Vedic hymn (i.91) the prayer:

> And Soma, let it be thy will
> For us to live, nor let us die...
> Thou Soma, bliss upon the old,
> And on the young and pious men
> Ability to live, bestowest.

Christ fulfilled "all the scriptures" — (cf. Luke 24:27) and gave "the best wine" — that inebriates one with love of God.

8. "The servants who had drawn the water"

Only the servants who had drawn the water knew from whence the wine had come. The steward and the bridegroom's friends were surprised that the best wine was kept to the last. Only the servants "knew," for they had done the work of filling those huge water pots. Only those who labor, who taste, who experience personally, really "know." "I am the taste of water." We read also in the Bhagavad Gita, "I am the knowledge of those who know" (10.38) and again, "I am the soul which dwells in the heart of all things" (10.20). "He is the Lord of all, who is hidden in the heart of all things. Those who know Him through their hearts and minds become immortal."[19] Immortality is given to those who have the knowledge that comes from having drunk of this "immortal nectar." And only those who labor at "drawing" from His Heart, in the cave of their own hearts, in meditation, know from whence comes this best wine, which alone can satisfy man's thirst forever.

John, whenever dealing with water (as in 1:26; 3:25; 4:10; 7:38), shows it to be both purifying and satisfying of thirst. The Cana miracle illustrates, as already seen, "at once the poverty of the old dispensation with its merely ceremonial cleansing and the richness of the new, in which the Blood of Christ is available both for cleansing (1:29) and for drink" (6.53). The initial reference is to the supersession of Judaism, but Bultmann is right to generalize: "The water stands for everything that is a substitute for revelation, everything by which a man thinks he can live, and which yet fails him when put to the test."[20]

Conclusion

And through water "his disciples came to believe in Him" (Jn. 2:11)

Thus, by working this miracle of transformation with his humble creature water, Jesus "manifested his glory." "The miracle of water made into wine may in itself not appear to be an apt indication of Christ's glory; however, it must be taken as John takes it, as the first of a series, all of which are related to the life that is to be found in the word of God."[21] "And his disciples came to believe in Him" — through water turned into wine. And we, too, come to believe that the water of the self — the *ahamkar* or ego — if poured out in silent, unresisting surrender like Mary's — can become, at her word of intercession, the wine of the Self, who dwells in the heart of all things.

> Be praised, my Lord,
> through sister water,
> for greatly useful, lowly,
> precious, chaste is she.
> St. Francis of Assisi

CHAPTER THREE

Waters of Rebirth

John 3:1-15

Unless a man is born through water and the Spirit, he cannot enter the Kingdom of God. (John 3:5)

Water, in which Jesus had himself been baptized, is now mentioned by Jesus to Nicodemus in connection with baptism of the Spirit. This Jewish rabbi, a Pharisee, had come to see Jesus surrpetitiously by night because of the official opposition to Jesus. The night is used perhaps symbolically, too — as in John 13:30 — to signify the night of his spiritual darkness. Nicodemus comes to seek light from Jesus, as though he were saying, *"Tamasoma Jyotirgamaya"*.[1]

"Rabbi," he said, "we know you are a teacher who comes from God; for no one can perform the signs that you do unless God were with him." Jesus shows Nicodemus that indeed He is from God, but in a way that he has not understood. The Kingdom of God is not to be seen merely through impressive miracles. It can only be experienced through a spiritual rebirth within oneself, "for the Kingdom of God is within you" (or "among you" — *entes humon* (Luke 17:21).

31

1. A spiritual rebirth

Without this spiritual rebirth, a man cannot enter the Kingdom. The "Kingdom" is a term used by the Synoptics, generally replaced by "Eternal Life" in John. Life always involves a birth. Since this is eternal life, it must involve a spiritual birth "from above" (cf. 1:12 f.). As happens frequently in Johannine dialogues, the expression is obscure enough to permit Nicodemus' retort: "How can a grown man be born?"

Nicodemus takes Jesus' enigmatic remark in a literal, physical sense. We may find it rather surprising and ironical that a rabbi should be puzzled by this figure of a rebirth since they used that expression for proselytes to Judaism, though, of course, the rebirth of which Jesus spoke goes beyond Judaism. However, unlike many other Pharisees and rabbis or doctors of law, Nicodemus is at least humble enough to know that he does not know. He asks for enlightenment, thereby not earning the condemnation by Jesus of those Jews whom he called "blind" because they thought they knew. "If you were blind, you would not be guilty, but since you say 'we see,' your guilt remains (Jn. 9:41). "Can he go back into his mother's womb and be born again?" asks Nicodemus. Jesus answers that man must be reborn "through water and the Spirit" — alluding to baptism and its necessity.

2. "Water and the Spirit"

We have already seen[2] how from the very beginning of the Bible there seems to have been a "marriage" between water and the Spirit. Here, however, it seems to come to a head, as it were. Bultmann, among others, seems to think that "water and" is here an "ecclesiastical" interpolation to give the text a sacramental meaning. Yet "there is no textual evidence for such an opinion and it must be rejected in view of the obvious structure of the Gospel; however, it is possible to think that John, in the light of his later Christian knowledge, has made the addition to Jesus' words concerning birth by the Spirit. John was evidently thinking of Christian baptism and expected his Christian readers to do the same."[3]

Already the Baptist had said, "I baptize with water, but there stands among you unknown to you — the one who is coming after me . . . the one who is going to baptize with the Holy Spirit" (Jn. 1:27, 33). That mankind may be born of the Spirit was the whole purpose of Jesus' coming. Already in the Old Testament, Messianic times were spoken of in terms of water and a new Spirit in man. "I shall pour clean water over you and you will be cleansed — I will . . . put a new spirit in you . . ." (Ex. 36:25). He can put His Spirit in us only if we are cleansed by the purifying waters. Would Nicodemus, accustomed to the water baptism of the Jews, of the Baptist in particular, have realized that to those water baptisms which at best were purificatory, must be added a Spirit baptism, vivificatory? Good though they were, those old religious rites remained in the sphere of things "natural" — things of "earth and flesh,"[4] things so lauded in our day as "perfectly beautiful," and so, in fact, they often are. But here Jesus shows that to them must be added a new thing, a thing "from above" of fire and spirit. Then the "streams of water" will flow — as will the "eschatological waters."

To be born anew — what is it, if not to be restored and purified? True, it means much more. To be born "from above" is far higher than mere restoration. Yet the theme of water holds an important place in the perspective of restoration of the people of God and may be worth casting a glance at this aspect first. After the gathering together of all the dispersed, God will distribute in abundance the purifying waters which will clean the heart of man and enable him to fulfill completely the law of Yahweh — with a new spirit — God's spirit. "Streams of water will flow from every mountain and every hill" (Is. 30:25), and all people will receive this spirit — men, women, servants (Joel 2:29). "There will be plenty of water for all the streams of Judah and a stream will flow . . ."

Flowing waters restore the spirit of man. Flowing water is probably an allusion to the legend in which the stream of water coming out of Eden (Gen. 2:10-14) that had been stopped by Adam's sin, reappeared again in the desert during the Exodus. The water flowed from the rock in twelve streams and finally reappeared in eschatological Jerusalem in one stream.[5]

God would work, then, more striking wonders than ever before — if before he had, by the hand of Moses, caused water to spring from the rock (Exod. 19:1-7; Num. 20:1-3, etc.). "He would make streams

pass through the wilderness, make rivers flow in the desert to give water
to my chosen people" (Is. 43:19).

In the light of all this overflowing generosity of God, it seems
intelligible that to be born of water and spirit means that "one cannot
become a Christian by birth but only by Rebirth." And "Christianity,"
as Ratzinger put it, "only ever comes into being by man's turning his
life round, turning away from the self-satisfaction of mere existence
and being 'converted.' In this sense baptism remains as the start of a
life-long conversion, the fundamental pattern of the Christian
existence... But if Christianity is regarded not as a chance grouping
of men but as the about-turn into real humanity, then the profession
of faith goes beyond the circle of the baptized and means that man does
not come to himself if he simply abandons himself to his natural center
of gravity. To become truly a man he must oppose this inclination, he
must turn round: even the waters of his nature do not climb upward
of their own accord."[6]

3. Born of the Spirit

It is God's spirit and His gratuitous gift of love which turns man
round — or, as Chesterton might have said, "upside down." (And indeed
isn't that precisely what Christ came to do and did — viz., turned all
the values of the world and man, who held them, "upside down"?)
If this seems impossible, it was as improbable as God making rivers
flow in the desert. It seems improbable or impossible to man but not
to the Holy Spirit. This is what Christ meant by "what is born of the
flesh is flesh; what is born of the Spirit is spirit (Jn. 3:6). The Spirit
is the principle of new life that Jesus has come to give, of which he
speaks to Nicodemus (Jn. 3:5-8), and which is operative by virture of
his glorification (cf. Jn. 7:38-9; Jn. 3:24; 4:13), for it is by the power
of the Spirit that the barrier of death is broken, and a definitive future
opened up for men and the world through Christ's Resurrection. But
— and this is what man finds very difficult to accept or remember —
before such a resurrection a person has to be turned "round-about"
or "upside down." There has first to be a death. Are we not baptized
into His death? Baptism means dying with Christ and rising with Him,

that becoming like Him in death we may attain the resurrection from the dead (cf. Phil. 3:10 f.). This is to be born of the Spirit.

4. Rebirth — "from death to life"

If we can think of Nicodemus coming by night to Jesus asking Him to lead him, as it were, "from darkness to light," Jesus shows him, as the Brihad Upanishad puts it, that it is the same as being led "from death to life." This Upanishadic prayer can only be fulfilled by water and the Spirit. "I have found the small path known of old that stretches far away. By it the sages who know the Spirit arise to the regions of heaven and thence beyond to liberation." The immersion — going down into the waters of baptism — and rising — coming out of them — is symbolic of the death-resurrection. It is the path of knowing the Spirit, which leads to true liberation.[7] This "passage" is the rebirth "by water and spirit." The solemn administration of baptism is essentially linked with the celebration of Easter Eve; baptism is a paschal sacrament, the sacrament of a person's "pass over" or *transitu paschalis* from death to life, from sin and the "old man" to the resurrection and the new man in Christ.[8] "Unless a man is born through water and the Spirit" means essentially this. Death, a problem which causes man such anguish, is resolved by the simple negation of the terms of the problem. In the Katha Upanishad one sees Yama, the God of death himself, teaching Nachiketas this lesson when he asks him to reveal what is beyond death. It is a remarkable fact that only Death is capable of teaching about death, revealing its insubstantiality. In Christian theology Jesus Himself also had to confront death. The living one is at once the "first-born of all creation" and the "first-born from the dead" (Col. 1:15-19).[9]

This passing from death to life is akin, again, to the seed being buried in the ground. "Unless the grain of wheat falling into the ground die," said Jesus elsewhere, "it remains alone, but if it dies, it brings forth much fruit" (Jn. 12:24).

This passing from death to life is again like a child having to hide for a while in the darkness of its mother's womb, if it is to be born. The womb is, too, like the tomb that holds in its dark embrace the body that will be awakened to life. We shall see a little more in detail later

how Nicodemus' seemingly naive question then is really a very preg-
nant one: "Can a grown man go back into his mother's womb and be
born again?" (Jn. 3:4) The whole man lies hidden in the womb, hidden
yet manifest. As at this entry into life man has to lie hidden in the womb,
at his departure from life, he has to lie hidden in the tomb, as a prelude
to entry into new life. It may be a tomb of earth, as when man is buried,
or it may be a watery tomb, as when he is put into a sacred river. The
mode matters little. The dying entails pain and fear, like the feeling
one may experience when wanting to enter a cave.

5. "The cave of the heart"

The Upanishads have a beautiful phrase — "dwelling in the cave
of the heart" — to express the Lord's abiding in man. To understand
truly the mystery of baptism of water — and the Spirit, one has to enter
the cave experience. This means entering into the thick darkness, the
frightening "unknownness," the unwelcoming darkness. It is under-
standable why so many saints and mystics of all religious traditions loved
meditating in caves. Even today in the caves of the Himalayan foothills,
one sees men entering into communion with God, with a certain freedom
and joy — unknown perhaps to those who have never entered to pray
in a cave. It may be of interest to read how one such saint came, through
his cave experience, to understand the presence and the word of God
within himself. Thus we read how Francis went each day into the cave
outside Assisi, after hearing the voice of Christ at Spoleto.

"Softly speaking into the dark cave's ear, Francis experienced the
parched joy of release. The protective shield of dark made it easier to
whisper hushed secrets into the emptiness. Every day it became harder
to leave his cave and meet the harsh light of all the staring world. The
farther into the cave he retreated, the more comfortably insulated he felt.

> "Lord Jesus, let me stay here; let me hide in the womb of this
> wet earth sponging me in soft, gentle mud." But every day he was
> driven outside again by the panic that the light would not be there
> to blind him. "O womb of earth, hide me from eyes that freeze
> me into this paralyzing fear." [Note: "the womb" of earth]

It was in the cave that Francis met Jesus and saw him for the first time. Up to that time his voices and dreams always seemed to come from without. . . but during the agonizing hours in the cave, he began to hear a voice inside himself, a deeper, clearer voice that was like discovering a part of himself he did not know was there. The more he prayed and turned to Christ for inspiration, the deeper he plunged toward some inner force that gave him strength and peace.

At first this inner search was a painful and terrifyng look at himself, at his weakness and sinfulness, and the journey was a downward dive that made him feel that he was drowning in some vast, bottomless lake. But as he persevered in prayer, he came at last to something like a great, silent waterproof cavern in which the sound of his own voice seemed hollow and deep, and there at that depth within, Jesus spoke softly to him and made his heart burn with love.[10]

It is interesting to note that until the time Francis entered the cave, his voices and dreams seemed to come from without. Now "in the agonizing hours in the cave," he became conscious of the presence of a voice within himself. This is the great discovery the baptized Christian, as indeed any Godseeker, has to make, that the God of heaven and earth dwells within the human heart.

"He who knows all and sees all, whose glory the universe shows, dwells as the Spirit of the divine city of Brahma (Brahmapur) in the region of the human heart" (Mundaka Up. 2.7) and again: "In the supreme golden chamber is Brahman, indivisible and pure" (v. 9).

Whether His abode in man is described in the Upanishads as "city," "chamber," or "cave," the important thing for us is that this is perhaps the keenest of all intuitions of the Indian rishis hundreds of years before Christ — and can become truly intelligible and luminous in the light of what Jesus came to offer man, through the baptism of water and spirit, and in turn throw new light on the words of the Gospel and on baptism. For truly, is this not the most tremendous thing that happens to us in baptism — that the Lord, who "dwells in the highest heavens," comes to live also "in the cave of the heart" (e.g., Jtaittiriya Upanishad 2.1)? For it is only when God is seen in his immanence as well as transcendence, that the knots of the heart are unloosened, the doubts of the mind vanish, and the laws of karma work no more (Mundaka Up. 2.8).

It is true that theologians may argue about the differences in the modes of God's presence in the heart of man before and after baptism, but god's presence is greater than all theologies (and later we shall speak of the sacrament and its effects). However, in the past, when baptism was taught, much more was made of sin being washed away by the waters of baptism than this entry into the soul of the Lord of glory. That purifying waters do cleanse away sin is true, as was and is believed both by the Jews and Hindus, but it is washed away precisely as a concomittant of God's life entering in. And the measure of growth of a Christian, one might say, is the measure of his consciousness of this true life within, in the cave of the heart. Could one not say, then, that to be born of water and the Spirit is this entry into the Kingdom of God within?

6. Entry and departure — baptism and *sannyas:*

This entry is akin to the *Sannyasi*'s descent into the holy river at his *Sannyas diksha*, symbolizing his entry into the *Brahma-Loka*. It is for him, as for a Christian at baptism, both an entry into a new life and a departure or death, "with no return." As he goes down, like the neophyte going down into the baptismal waters, it is an act of renunication that he makes. *Sannyas* means "perfect renunciation" [*Sam* — "perfect"; *nyasa* — "abandoning or setting aside"]. True, at baptism, except perhaps in some adult baptism, one does not renounce the world as a would-be monk renounces it, in direct response to his burning desire for God, through *mumukhutva*, his longing for liberation. And at first sight it may surprise one to see a comparison drawn between baptism — which is the first sacrament of initiation into Christian life — and *Sannyasa* — which is the last of the fours stages or *Ashrama* in a Hindu's life, by which he leaves his famly, possessions, and all — knowing from life experience that what is permanent cannot be attained through what is impermanent (cf. Kathopanishad 4.1). Yet, on closer examination, one sees an intimate connection between baptismal initiation by water and spirit, and *Sannayasa-diksha*, likewise given by water and spirit.

For to become a Christian means to accept the challenge of Jesus! "What does it profit a man to gain the whole world, but suffer the loss of his own soul?" (Mk. 8:36) or "If any man follow me, let him deny

(renounce) himself, take up his cross daily and follow Me'' (Lk. 9:23).
It is precisely his ''self'' that he has to renounce when the follower
of Christ knowingly accepts the responsibilities of his baptism. In
renouncing his ''self'' he gives up all. For nothing but the Kingdom
of Heaven has in itself an absolute value to which all else should be
sacrificed. The Gospel is incompatible with half measures, and only
when it loses its savor can Christianity be turned into a comfortable
religion.[11] ''Do you renounce Satan and all his works and pomps?''
the neophyte is relevantly asked. So, too, true *Sannyas*, as the Gita is
later to insist, is not so much leaving the world to practice austerities
in the forest (cf. Mudaka Up. 1.2.11-13) as to renounce one's lower
self, so as to find one's true Self — the *Atman* or the Spirit within —
the Self beyond the ego. He turns his back once and for all on his ''self''
in order to enter the life of the Self and thereby to be fully free.

And so the Christian guru might say to the new *sannyasi* at ''the
great departure with no possible return'' — in Abhishiktanandji's words:

> Go my son, in the freedom of the Spirit
> across the infinite space of the heart,
> Go to the source, go to the Father,
> Go to the unborn, yourself unborn [*ajatha*]
> to the Brahma Loka
> which you yourself have found
> and from which there is no returning.
> *Na punaravartate*[12]

Thus there is a deep and striking similarity between the descent
into the waters of an initiate for baptism and that of a *sannyaasi* taking
his *diksha*. Both enter the waters to be initiated into the freedom of the
Spirit, to be ''born anew.''

Though this parallelism between *sannaayasa diksha* and baptism
is very interesting, perhaps it should be noted, too, that there is naturally
also a difference — renunciation of the world and commitment to it.
While baptism is a distinct religious act vis-a-vis renunciation of sin
and the ''old man,'' it is renunciation of ''the world'' in the Johannine
sense — ''the world'' as opposed to the Spirit. If it is a renunciation
it is also and primarily an initiation rite into a new society — more
comparable in significance if not in rite to the thread or Upanayana

ceremony. Also while the *sannyasi* abandons society, to live hidden
and unknown, to "stand steadfast in the secret place of the heart," the
newly baptized commits himself to live in and for society, and "born
anew" as he is, as a member of the Society of Christ's mystical Body.
It is interesting and significant, too, that while the *sannyasi* immerses
himself in the waters, the catechumen is dipped into them by someone
else — perhaps indicative that the latter is thereby initiated into a group,
while the former leaves all society and wanders away into the unknown.

7. "Journey downwards"

This great discovery of one's true Self in the depth of one's self
can only be made by man at the cost of this "journey downward," this
departure or dying, this "painful and frightening dive" into the waters,
into the cave, into the womb. Only so can man be "reborn" to the Life
of God within. "Thus, and no otherwise." The waters, the cave, the
womb — all have one thing in common. They all require man to lower
himself, to become little, to go down.

8. The Guha and the womb

Twice in the description of Francis' entry into the cave (given
above), "the womb of earth" is mentioned. The word *womb*, as we
have seen, is used by Nicodemus in his questioning of Jesus: "How
can a man be born again? Can he enter into his mother's womb?" It
is precisely this that he has to do, insists Jesus. "Unless you become
as little children, you cannot enter the Kingdom of Heaven" (Matt. 18:3).
"It is to such as they that the Kingdom of Heaven belongs" (Matt.
19:14). Indeed, one shuld "accept the Kingdom as a little child" (Mk.
10:15). The secret of true grandeur is to make oneself little, like a child,
and practice true humility in order to become a son of the heavenly
Father. He must "return to the state of childhood" — even unto being
like an as-yet-unborn babe — totally dependent and weak in the womb
of its mother — helpless and hidden. God, too, chooses then to "hide"
in the cave or womb of man's heart! O, mystery of mysteries!

This idea of the cave and the womb, in which is hidden the Lord of Life, is found linked in India, both in her mythology and in her scripture. In the Kena Upanishad one sees the absolute necessity of being little and humble if one is to see God. Thus Vayu, the God of wind, and Agni, the God of fire, both do not recognize Brahman because of their pride in attributing their victory to their own powers. The *devas* fail to recognize him. And even to Indra, the God of thunder, he reveals himself only in the act of disappearing, and that, too, through the intervention of a "lady radiant in beauty."

"Then in the same region of the sky the God saw a lady of radiant beauty." She was Uma, divine wisdom, the daughter of the mountains of snow. "Who is that being that fills us with wonder?" he asked. "He is Brahman, the Spirit Supreme," she answered. "Rejoice in him, since through him you attained the glory of victory" (Kena Up., parts 3 & 4).

It is rather like Mary, the Queen of Beauty and Seat of Wisdom, through whose intervention God-made-man was introduced to the lowly shepherds, the wise men (wise because humble) and the wedding party in Cana, whose wine ran out and who knew "their utter need of God."[13]

The Supreme Lord was hidden, yet manifest. He is rightly described as *guhahita, guhasaya, guhacare* ("abiding, resting, moving in secret") — in "the secret place of the heart." He has entered into the hidden place [Kathop 1.29 — *gudham anupravistah*]. This theme of entering, descending, being hidden yet present — also corresponds to that of birth. Thus the *guha* (cave) becomes the maternal womb.

"In the waters, O Lord, is your womb" (Satpatha Brahaman IV 8.2.4)

"In the waters, O Lord, is your seat" (Rig. Ved. VIII 4.3.9)

Prajapati moves about within the "womb" (Maha Narayana Up. 1.11; ff. Prayapatiscarati garbhe antah).

He is born endlessly, he was born and will be born again, he is born and diffused. "He is the unique, the one eternally born and born in everything that is born, and paradoxically he is *'a-ja'*, the not-born. At the level of manifestation he is born and dies; at the level of his inner mystery, he simply is and the discovery, the realization, of this is salvation, *mukti*[14].

All the mystics — both of East and West — who have entered the waters, the cave, the womb, have been "reborn" to this discovery, this realization. This is the new life — their salvation. And to make it more intelligible and possible for man, God-made-man "at the level of manifestation" also was born, died and rose again to His life of Being. He always was; for He Is; *asti* — "at the level of His inner mystery." In the rite for the blessing of baptismal water on Holy Saturday, the Church prays: ". . . may a heavenly offspring, conceived in holiness and reborn into a new creation, come forth from the stainless womb of this divine font." Invoked during the baptism ceremony, the Lord who was born, died, and rose again, fills this water in the font with the power of His Holy Spirit and fructifies it, so that it may beget new life in the Church.

9. Sacramental waters

No wonder the fathers, from Tertullian on, call this "washing of water with the 'word,'" a *Sacramentum* or *Mysterium*, a term they also used for other sacred acts. By the third or fourth century the word had permanently acquired this technical sense. "Baptism is sacrament, an initiation that involves swearing fidelity in the service of Christ. . . But *sacramentum* also was a sacred act that communicated symbolically what it represented, and molded the believers to its likeness. As image of the death and resurrection of Christ, the mystery made the believer participate in the passover of Christ from death to life."[15] Thus *sacramentum* meant both oath and mystery — two distinct meanings.

The symbolism of water then finds its complete meaning in Christian baptism. As we have seen, from its start in the biblical tradition, water was used at baptism because of its cleansing value, just as in the Hindu tradition for the same reason it was used for holy baths and sippings and all other sacramental acts, from the initiation to the death ceremonies. John baptized with water "for the remission of sins" (Matt. 3:11), using for this purpose the water of the same river (the Jordan) — in which Naaaman the leper had been cleansed (2 Kings 5:10-14). But baptism brings about the cleansing not of the body, but of the soul, or the "conscience" (1 Peter 3:21). It is a bath that cleanses us from our sins (1 Cor. 6:11; Eph. 5:26; Heb. 10:22; Acts 22:16). And to this basic symbolism of baptismal water, as Boismard points out,[16] Paul added, as we have seen, another — the immersion and emerging of the neophyte

(Rom. 6:3-11). Perhaps Paul here envisioned in the water of baptism an image of the sea, dwelling place of malevolent powers and symbol of death, overcome by Christ just as formerly the Red Sea was overcome by Yahweh(1 Cor. 10 f., Is. 51:10). Baptism is thought of, then, as a bath of rebirth and renewal of the Holy Spirit; for as we have seen, it is also a principle of new life — Life in the Spirit. For parallel to the very Pauline theology of baptism into the death of Christ, another conception looms even larger — the impregnation of baptismal water with the sanctifying power of Christ's spirit.

10. Theology of baptism

The early theological thought, this impregnation of baptismal water, meant the water washing away our old mortality (sin) and the ascent from the water was the passage from death to life (cf. Pseudo Barnabas, Shepherd of Hermas). It transports us from over the frontier of death into the life of Christ (St. Clement). . . Origen, as usual, upholds the primacy of the interior, spiritual order over the outward and visible. He further stresses that the person being baptized must seek practical understanding of what baptism signifies. Baptism means, as we have seen, renunciation, conversion, penance. It completes sacramentally the ascetical death of the catechumen; but "if anyone," says Origen, "comes to the washing of water (continuing) in sin, then his sins are not remitted" (21st Homily on Luke).

In the classical patriotic age — fourth and fifth centuries — the theology of baptism reached maturity. In the scholastic age it was systematized. "The Tridentine Decrees were merely designed to set down and secure the traditional faith concerning baptism. Within their framework we must try to grasp the positive truth in full measure; it will not do to repeat anathemas. Such, however, was the tendency of theologians in the ensuing age. Understandably enough, the remarkable achievements of Trent had the effect in practice of narrowing their field of vision. But today the situation is quite different. Not only the exigencies of ecumenical dialogues, but the new vitality that is stirring due to liturgical reform and deeper study of God's work, impel us to

recast our theology of baptism in an ampler mold, taking full account
of scripture (both biblical and nonbiblical), liturgical experience and
experiments, the storehouse of patristic, scholastic theology, as well
as the best we can cull from the theologies of other religions.[17]

11. Conscious Christians — "Now, not I"

True, today, baptismal waters are poured out in a few drops, and
that, too, generally over a child — something that many understandably
question, for how can the child "seek practical understanding of what
baptism signifies?" And how many parents, godparents, or educators
take their full responsiblity of seeing that as it grows to maturity, the
child's comprehension and obligations of baptism, which the infant did
not have, are given gradually and adequately to it? Yet, from the fourth
and fifty centuries onward, infant baptism developed naturally and was
a sort of appendage to the baptism of adults, which was always the main
concern. Today, in post-Christian or non-Christian countries and times,
it would again seem appropriate to think more of adult baptism. Nevertheless, the rite of Baptism, even as it is, embodies the faith which the
"living waters" bring and symbolize. It is more than just a "symbolic"
expression of faith; it is a real access to Christ, a dying and rising with
Him so that becoming like Him in His death, we may attain the resurrection from the dead (cf. Phil. 3.10 f.) Though the outward form of
the present baptismal liturgy of the Latin Church may not be altogether
appropriate, it proclaims clearly enough what baptism is since its origin
in the New Testament. In Baptism, then, the Church possesses something
alive and operative, though it is not always understood by the recipients
of the sacramental waters. Perhaps it would be good if we went back
to the long, remote, and thorough preparation of the candidate as in
the early times, with an immediate preparation of fasting, prayer, and
promises; then the solemnity of baptism itself — an actual bath in flowing
water, in which the candidate is immersed thrice — like the Hindu
sannyasi — knowing what and why he is "renouncing" Satan and all
his works and pomps. Then out of the waters of baptism may rise up
Christians who "know in whom they have believed" — ready to
renounce themselves, i.e., lay down their lives day by day, or if need
be, once and for all, as did their Founder and Lord.

Such Christians would know, then, that this descent into and ascension from the waters, this dying and rising, means a commitment to the person of Jesus Christ; that through, with, and in him, they can "pass over" to the Father, whom "no man has seen at any time," at the level of His inner mystery. They would know that thus they enter deep, through the cave of His Heart and through the water that flowed from that crucified Heart, into the Trinitarian life of God — and become "one" with it — even as a drop of water merges into the ocean and becomes one with it. This simile of water is one that Christian mystics like St. Teresa of Avila, Catherine of Sienna and others were not afraid to use. Then the Christian who has passed through baptismal waters can truly say without fear and in joy, as did St. Catherine of Genoa, "My me is God"; or with St. Paul, "I live now, not I, but Christ lives in me."

Fergus Kerr, O.P. describes what this means realistically: "In principle the transition from Christ as memory, to Christ as present fact, takes place in the soul of each baptized person — in whom Christ dies and rises, and who dies and rises in Christ. The task is to make conscious this prodigious psychological revolution."[18]

Thus being born through "water and the Spirit," men and women with understanding and faith can — as Nicodemus slowly learned "by night," enter the Kingdom of God. The language of birth and rebirth — common in Hellenistic religions (which, when John was writing offered rebirth to men) — was used by the Evangelist, as we have seen, for his sacramental theology. But this new rebirth of the Spirit would also give those who accepted it in faith freedom of the Spirit.

12. "Freedom of the Spirit"

Jesus says to Nicodemus, "Do not be surprised because I tell you that you must all be born again. The wind blows wherever it wishes; you hear the sound it makes, but you do not know from where it comes or where it is going. It is like that with everyone who is born of the Spirit" (Jn. 3:8). Christ uses an analogy which involves a play on words. Both in Aramaic and Greek the same word means "spirit," "breath," and "wind." And who can control the wind or say from where it comes or whither it goes? "As the wind, though one, takes new forms in all things that live" (Katha Up. 5.10). Or who can say when man's breath

will begin or end his life? It is free. And when it stops, his life ceases.
The Spirit is to man's spiritual life what breath is to his physical life.
The Breath of Life is sovereign and supremely free.

Thus *Ruah* (Aramaic) and *Pneuma* (Greek) would be equivalent
to *Shakti* in India, or in Vedic terminoloty, *Prana*. It is interesting to
see its role in the light of what Christ teaches us of Life in the Spirit.
Prana refers primarily to the Source of Life within and its diffused
appearance throughout all the organs of the body and mind, which are
called *Pranah* or vital breaths in the plural. As when a ruler commands
his officials and appoints them cities to be ruled, even so, *Prana*, the
power of life, rules the other ruling powers of the body'' (Prasna Up.
3.4). "The powers of life adore the God who is in the heart and he
rules the breath of life, breathing in and breathing out. . .''

> A mortal lives not through that breath that flows in and that flows
> out. The source of his life is Another and this causes the breath
> to flow [Katha Up. 5.3-5]

In the later Indian context, Spirit of God would be understood as
the most intimate core of the conscious being, at the level beyond the
reach of sense or mind, as meaning his *atman*, his self, since he is the
deepest center, the very "inwardness" of the divine mystery.[19] He is
the Breath of our breath. To know this one *Atman* was to want to abandon all other discourse, and to realize that "This Atman is Brahman"
(Brihad Up. 3.4.4). The same Spirit, the Holy Spirit, is this very
"Inwardness" of Christ. His "Self," the *Atman*, the breath, is given
to us, through water and the same Spirit — to be our very Inwardness,
and thus enable us to participate in the very life of Christ and of His
Father.

If, as Dodd says, the whole of chapter three of St. John is concerned
with the idea of initiation into eternal life (or rebirth)[20], then the eighth
verse tells us the kind of freedom that persons initiated into God's life
would possess. Born of the Spirit, they are free like the wind — the
"knots" of their hearts are unloosed; they are not dependent on others'
ideas, criticism, approvals; they find their happiness in Him whom they
have grown to love as their very Self, to know as the Breath of their
very life, as of the Trinitarian life within them. They are moved by

the Spirit alone, they go where His wind fills their souls. They speak
— as did Christ — only what the Father, through His Spirit, wants them
to speak, for they are filled with the Spirit. The one whom God has
sent speaks God's words, because God gives him the fullness of His
Spirit (Jn 3:34). And whoever "believes," whom God has sent and
who speaks His words, has "eternal life; he has it already in this world"
(cf. 3:36). It is only through faith that the baptismal waters can give
us this life in (of) the Spirit.

13. Whoever believes in the Son

"None of you is willing to accept our message," says Jesus. "You
do not believe me when I tell you about heavenly things" (Jn. 3:11-12).
"Whoever believes in the Son is not judged" (v. 18) reiterates the
classical verse 16: "God so loved the world that he gave his only Son,
so that everyone who believes in Him may have eternal life." It is worthy
of note that it is believing in Him — not mere baptism — that gives
eternal life. Thus Jesus, when commending his disciples to go and baptize
all men, does not say "who is not baptized will be condemned" — as
many thought or may still — but rather — "whoever believes and is
baptized will be saved — whoever does not *believe* will be condemned"
(Mk. 16:16), i.e., those who consciously and deliberately reject Him.
Faith brings rebirth and gives entrance to eternal life — as Marsh so
rightly says when commenting on "and this is the judgment". . . or the
"condemnation" (v. 19). The Evangelist makes it plain that it is a reflex
of the act of God's love that people may condemn themselves, and not
a separate and posterior act of God's judicial condemnation. Even this
judgment speaks His love. The "condemnation" is then[21] the reverse
side of God's love when man deliberately rejects God's offer of love.
   This is reiterated in the last words of the chapter, v. 31 ff., (which
are "imprecise" — as to whether they were spoken by Jesus, by the
Evangelist or by the Baptist) — referring to his testimony that Jesus
was the Lamb, the Son of God (Jn. 1:29-34). Yet they bring out clearly
that "No one accepts his message (v. 32) though He comes from above"
and "though he who comes from heaven is above all" (v. 31).

Conclusion

This statement moves now to the crucial summary of what the dialogue between Jesus and Nicodemus amounts to. It is this: The one whom God has sent, Jesus the great apostle, speaks the words of God. Of this we may be sure because the Father has not given the Spirit to the Son in any stinted measure but without measure at all. The Father indeed loves the Son (3:16; 1:18) and has given everything into his hand. That is to say, as the following explanatory verse makes plain, the whole issue of human life and its destiny, the whole question of eternal life or death, is involved in man's answer to what the Son says (v. 24) — the Son to whom "God had given the fullness of His Spirit" (3:34).

So it was not merely the waters and "the ritual washing" about which soon afterwards John's disciples began arguing with a few people when John was baptizing in Aenon "because there was plenty of water in that place" (Jn. 3:23-30). It was, rather, a matter of recognizing, as did the Baptist, Him on whom the Spirit had descended in his fullness, and like the Baptist, being willing to become lowly, little, nothing, that He may be all in him. "He must become more important while I become less important"; something only the Spirit can achieve in man — through the waters flowing over him in baptism. To want to decrease in importance can only become possible to a man who has learned the all-absorbingness of God's love and presence within, who has, therefore, had the courage to descend into the cave, the womb, the water. Only then he begins to care little or nothing for man's compliments and companionship. He yearns more and more to be considered little in their eyes, to disappear — in order all the more freely to enjoy the Presence within (cf. Jn. 14:23), in the cave of the heart.

"You know what this Presence means! Something quite different from the Creator's presence in His creature. By it, you contract a divine friendship, inducting you into an intimate relationship with the Trinity, now your Guest. The hermit sees this indwelling presence of God as the specific personal reasons for withdrawing into the desert. He comes here to live this divine truth, to the exclusion of all other occupations. In this, above all, his vocation is an eschatological one he begins on earth, in the shadows of faith, by the light of love, what he will be doing for all eternity."[22]

While it is not every man or woman who is called to withdraw into the desert and make the relishing of this Presence his sole occupation, it is, as St. John takes pains to make clear, every one's duty to learn to be aware of this Presence. He reiterates: "This is eternal life to know Thee..." (Jn. 17:3). Eternal life begins here and now. To be born "of water and the Spirit" means to know Him. "Those who know Him have found immortality" (Katha Up. 6.2) and with it already everything; for He is "that which, when known, all is known" (Mundaka Up. 1.1.3).

As rivers flowing into the ocean find their final peace, and their name and form disappear, even so the wise become free from name and form and enter into the radiance of the Supreme Spirit who is greater than all greatness. "In truth who knows God becomes God" (Mundaka Up. 3.2.8-9).

CHAPTER FOUR

Living Streams

John 4:1-30

The water that I shall give will turn into a spring inside him, welling up to eternal life. John 4:14

Water had provided a symbol for John to speak of purification — in "the waters of recognition" — when the Baptist saw the Spirit coming down on Jesus standing in the River Jordan (chapter one). Water had been instrumental in Jesus' performance of his first sign — turning water into wine (chapter two). It had been the symbol and means of initiation into the Christian life and community, as Jesus explained baptism "by water and the Spirit" to Nicodemus (chapter three). Now water is to be used to speak of continual renewal and growth in that life (chapter four). It is not enough that a trickle of water begins to flow from the hillside; it must go on flowing and increasing its velocity; it must continue to flow on — until it reaches its source again. Jesus was not to teach that the water He gives would not only slake the thirst of the would-be drinker, but turn him/her into a living stream — a *Jeevan-Dhara* — to slake others' thirst.

Leaving Judea for Galilee, He chose to pass through Samaria. Being tired, He sat down by Jacob's well, in a town called Sychar, "near

50

a field that Jacob had given to his son Joseph" (Gen. 33:19, 48:22).
"Being tired" — for Jesus was human — He "sat" — according to
one translation, "on the ground" rather than "at the well" — rather
like a tired man would sit by an Indian well.

Then followed a scene which is also very like that which could easily
occur in an Indian village. A woman comes to draw water, and Jesus
surprised her not only by talking to her — (speaking to a woman in
public was unheard of) — but also by asking her for a drink of water.
For a Jew to request water of a Samaritan was like a Brahmin asking
for water of a Harijan woman. Jesus shows himself to be above such
scruples over such man-made laws and again demonstrates his sovereign
freedom. That he chose to have this beautiful and God-revealing conversation with a woman "by the well" is of significance to us.

1. Wells and springs

In Israel — as in India — well-side meetings and conversations were
proverbial. "In the evening when women go down to draw water"!
(Gen. 24:11) A phrase such as that can conjure up all sorts of images
in an Indian mind: women's chatting and gossiping about someone's
misdemeanor or good fortune; the *gopis* watching Radha being
beleaguered by Krishna; the young man waiting for a tryst by the well
with his beloved; the parent of a would-be bride settling a dowry for
the marriage. Thus in the Bible — which deals with Orientals — we
read of Abraham's servant praying, "Here I stand by the spring as the
young women from the town come out to draw water. To one of the
girls I will say, 'Please fill your pitcher and let me drink.' If she answers,
'Drink, and I will water your camels too,' may she be the one you have
chosen for your servant Isaac" (Gen. 24:10 f.). So, too, in Genesis
29, we read of Jacob meeting Rachel, how he "kissed her and burst
into tears" (v. 2) near the well used for watering flocks of sheep. The
seven daughters of the priest of Midian came to draw water and fill
the troughs to water their father's sheep. When shepherds came to drive
them away, Moses came to their defense and "watered their sheep for
them" and one of them became Moses' wife (Exod. 2:16 ff).

Wells and springs play a significant part in the life and religion of the patriarchal and Exodus periods of the Old Testament. Thus Moses was told by Yahweh: "Strike the rock and water will flow from it for the people to drink" — for "the grumbling sons of Israel" who put Yahweh to the test (Exod. 17:1-7).[2] Jacob's well was of the usual sort, gathering its water by infiltration. It could thus be thought of as filled with running or living water, if it were compared with water that stood in hewn cisterns that collected nothing — just as it could be thought of as quite different if it were compared with the fresh, lively water that came rushing down the hillsides in the rainy season and fell into the gushing Ganges.

Philippe Reymond points out how "the waters of the deep below" were distinguished in the Old Testament from "the waters from above," and yet there is no explanation of why certain waters rise to the surface of the earth and others lie dormant like water in a well.[3]

In the Old Testament spring water symbolizes the life that God gives, especially that of the Messianic age. "You will draw waters joyfully from the springs of salvation" (Is. 12:3) could well have been in Christ's mind as he was fulfilling that prophecy to the Samaritan woman — once she recognized Him as the Giver and Source of living water and wanted to drink of it, but that took some time.

Apart from the symbolism of the watery place Jesus chose as the locale of the beautiful incident, it is wholly right and to be expected, as Marsh points out, that the Son incarnate in the flesh chose to raise the greatest spiritual questions by quite simple, physical, this-worldy acts, and what more simple and ordinary than water? John is able, too, through this incident, to forward the great themes of his Gospel — water, temple, etc.[4] It is of interest and typically Johannine, too, that he mentions that the well provides water for thirsty, weary man — whose "name and form" he chose to take — "at the sixth hour" — the very hour he was to make the same request from the cross — "I thirst" (Jn. 19:28). And just as now He gives "living water" to the woman at the well, which symbolizes the Spirit (cf. Jn. 7:39 — "He was speaking of the Spirit which those who believed in Him were to receive"), so then, after He had taken the drink on the cross, he was to bow His head and give up His spirit (Jn. 19:30). The last breath of Jesus was taken for the outpouring of the Spirit (cf. Jn. 1:33 f., 20:22, etc.). Water and the Spirit are ever inseparable in John's thought, as they were, indeed, in God's designs, from the very creation of the world.

2. "Give me to drink"

This simple request of Jesus for water again brings in questions of purification, with which the Gospel had been dealing ever since it mentioned for the first time the baptism of John — as if it cannot get away from man's constant need for purification. It is well known, too, that the closer a person comes to God, the more he feels his impurity near the all-pure, and the more ardently he feels his need for purifica- tion. Dr. Daube points out that the comment "You are a Jew and you ask me, a Samaritan, for a drink?" (v. 9) reflects a piece of regulation that regarded all Samaritan women as "menstruants from their cradle." Hence to drink from a common vessel with any one of them was for a Jew to incur uncleanness.[5] "For Jews in fact do not associate with Samaritans" (v. 10) — do not have dealings with Samaritans. Dr. Daube says the real meaning of this latter phrase is not "to have dealings with," but "use together with." These purification regulations about water, drinking from the same vessels with others of a different "caste" (as we would say in India), make this whole Gospel incident come truly alive and remind us of our everyday situation even today. Jesus could as easily have enacted this scene in a Harijan village of India as in Samaria. One recalls, too, the scene in K.A. Abbas' film *"Char Dil Char Raahen"* where Meena Kumari as a Harijan hesitantly offers water to Jairaj. And as Abbas rightly said, "The Harijan issue is an issue of Human Rights which cannot be regarded as an internal problem of India." It is as though Christ, knowing the universality of this problem, enacted this scene for all the world to know and understand that God who is One is the same God of all His children — and all are alike, dear to Him. (What a mystery and an enigma, what guilt and oppression of the poor, that water, so liberally given by God to man, is not available to millions in India and the third world, even today.) It shows, too, the new freedom and a largesse of spirit that Christ brings into the world. Impurities are not incurred by association with other "caste" people, or by what we eat and drink or through vessels used for this purpose. They are incurred by what is in man's heart and in his spirit. Jesus brings to the world a religion of the spirit — not of the law and the letter of the law,[6] as He is to show later about worship too.

The dialogue that follows makes this clear. For it is not merely at the level of a well-side conversation; a marriage fixed, a lover's tryst, a slaking of thirst. Yet, it is all these. The depth of a profound probing into the relationship between sinful man and a wooing God makes it all these and more. And water again becomes the witness, the occasion and an excuse or instrument, *nimitta-matra*, as the Gita would say. The real "agent of change" and "cause of bliss" is, as always, God alone.

3. Living water

Jesus says, "If you only knew the gift of God!" or "what God is offering," as the Jerusalem Bible translates it. For every request made by God is really an offer of a gift from Him. Here He offers the best of all His gifts, Himself — and the Holy Spirit — symbolized by the "living water" which he goes on to offer the woman. The phrase is a clear indication of the highly symbolic character of the narrative. Some think Jesus may have been referring to the law, the Torah, which both Jews and Samaritans claimed to honor. Though he was the weary and thirsty traveller, he could offer her refreshment and strength. Had she know or understood the Scriptures, she would have been able to recognize Him. But she did not know or understand any more than we do, and so she failed to grasp the significance of his great words: "If you only knew what God is offering and who it is that is saying to you, 'give me a drink,' you would have been the one to ask, and he would have given you living water" (Jn. 4:10).

In John one constantly finds terms which in addition to their obvious meaning appreciated by the audience, possess a metaphorical and higher sense[7] and it is really a question of "He that hath ears to hear, let him hear" and understand. The woman first takes it to mean running water as distinct from well or cistern water, but as Jesus explains, it means "water of life," a figure borrowed from the Old Testament (cf. Zech. 14:8, Prov. 13:14, etc.) where it signified divine vitality, revelation, wisdom.[8] "Living water," like the "gift of God" par excellence is, within Judaism, the Torah. In gnostic thought, too, it was the life-giving revelation. Fresh, flowing water, also creating and maintaining life, in the Old Testament stood for divine activity and quickened men to life — as long as they did not forsake Him, the fountain of living water, and go to "leaky cisterns" (Jer. 2:13). And wherever the river flowed out of Jerusalem, everything would live (Exod. 47:9). In Rabbinic literature, "living" water was not commonly used, but "water" was; sometimes standing for the Holy Spirit, more often for the Torah. In the Qumran the same usage is found; water gives life, cleanses. Philo speaks of the divine word as "full of the streams of wisdom."[9] And as Barret observes, the metaphor of water is less common in the West; in the waterless spaces of the East, the value of water is most apparent. Water stands prominently for the Holy Spirit, which gives life (Jn. 6:63), and again Jesus offers it, for it is he who will truly give what the law merely promised.

4. "You have no bucket, Sir"

Keeping on the physical level of water, the woman says, "Sir (she speaks with respect already, and soon will call him "prophet" and "Messiah"), "You have no bucket." How often we think God needs our man-made tools to do His work and even offer them to Him at times, and which, instead of laughing at us, He deigns to use. Such is the mystery of His outpoured Love! Not only does the woman — like Nicodemus before her — take his words literally, but she begins to recall history and passes on to religious issues — like so many who escape the crucial issues of life by discussing philosophy! Since Jesus cannot draw water from that deep well, from where could He get it? Is he "greater than our father Jacob?" (Jn. 4:12) The woman may be ironical at this stage, but she little knew how much "greater than Jacob" He really was.

Descending, as they claimed to do, from the patriarchs, the Samaritans, too, could say, "gave us this well." By these words the water of the well is qualified as "water of Judaism" (cf. 2:6). The woman cannot recall Deuteronomy 8:7 and so cannot understand the answer of Jesus in the following verse.

5. "A spring inside of Him"

"Whosoever drinks this water will get thirsty again; but anyone (anyone — not of any particular religion, race, caste) who drinks the water that I shall give will never be thirsty again; the water that I shall give will turn into a spring inside him, welling up to eternal life" (Jn. 4:13-14).

It had been written in Deuteronomy: "God is bringing you into a prosperous land of streams and of waters that well up from the deep in valleys and hills (Jn. 8:7). This is reminiscent of Genesis 49:25: "Shaddai, who blesses you with blessings of heaven above and blessings of the deep lying below," i.e., the subterranean waters that irrigate the earth. "The deep" here, however, is the heart — with a stream overflowing from the infinite Heart of God into "the cave of the heart" of man. What Jesus has to offer this woman is quite unparalleled in history. What he has to give man will infiltrate inside of him and become within him a spring of water. The religion Jesus offers is essentially one of the "inside," the interior — not of exteriorities — rites, rubrics, liturgies, observances, minutiae of the law — but of the Spirit, the *Atman*. The water He gives will slake man's thirst in such a way that he "will never be thirsty again." Man is made in such a manner that he has an infinite capacity for knowing, loving, and for giving happiness; for being known, loved — and of receiving infinite happiness. Now only two things can make it possible for him to be satisfied. This is well put by the seers of Upanishadic times — and which lights up, as it were, this verse of John.

> He who knows Brahman as the Real, knowledge, infinite, hidden
> in the secret place of the heart and in the highest heaven, realizes
> all desires in communion with the all-knowing Brahman. (Taittiriya
> Up. 2.1.1)

He must "know" God — for knowledge of God above — Brahma-Vidya — can satisfy man completely and he must know Him "hidden in the cave of the heart."

Another lovely verse of the Katha Upanishad speaking of the one amid men who grants their desires says: "Only the wise who perceive

Him as abiding in the soul, attain eternal bliss, eternal peace; and no others'' (2.2.13).

This is the living water that ''turns into a spring inside him'' — and which alone can slake man's thirst completely and forever. Yet it is difficult for us — as for the Samaritan Woman — to see this and yet more, to act on it. So, like her, we remain on the level of the seen and felt. ''Sir, give me some of that water that I may never get thirsty, and never have to come here again to draw water'' (v. 15).

She is thinking of saving herself trouble. Little does she know how much more trouble it is for man to struggle to reach the water spring within. For man is prone to turn outwards and seeks all his satisfaction from sense gratification. Again, it is Katha Upanishad that describes this phenomenon exquisitely.

''The creator made the senses outward-going; they go to the world of matter outside, not to the Spirit within. But a sage who sought immortality looked within himself and found his own self. The foolish run after outward pleasures and fall into the snares of vast-embracing death. But the wise have found immortality, and do not see the Eternal in things that pass away'' (Kathop 4.1-2). This discerning ability — Vivek — is considered by Shankara, the first prerequisite of Brahma Vidya; the ability to distinguish between the permanent and the passing. Only then can a Nachiketes turn down all the alluring temptations of Yama (Kathop X), or a Maitreyi answer her husband Yajnavalkya, wanting before leaving for his forest days, to settle all his possessions upon her: ''If all the earth filled with riches belonged to me, O my Lord, should I thereby attain eternal life? . . . what should I then do with possessions that cannot give me life eternal? Give me instead your knowledge, O my Lord'' (Brihadaranyaka Up. 4.2.4).)

It is then this knowledge of the source within — the life of the Spirit alone that can give us full and complete happiness; and no other knowledge: ''Know that Brahman is forever in thee and nothing higher is there to be known'' (Svetasvatara Up. 1.12).

6. In spirit and in truth

Jesus now tries something else with the woman. He asks her to call her husband. And when she says, ''I have no husband,'' he shows

her that he has superhuman knowledge. "You are right to say 'I have
no husband,' for though you have had five, the one you have now is
not your husband" (v. 18).[10] For once she is stumped. She accosts her
own reality in which Jesus encounters her: "Many lovers, no husband."
All she can say is, "I see you are a prophet, Sir," and to save herself
further embarrassment, perhaps, tries to divert the conversation into
safer channels — theoretical talk about religious worship! What would
the prophet say regarding the long-standing controversy between Jews
and Samaritans over the right place for sacrificial worship? Jesus answers
that soon such a question will have no more relevance — neither in
the temple nor on this mountain!

"True worshippers will worship the Father in spirit and in truth;
that is the kind of worshipper the Father wants. God is spirit and those
who worship must worship in spirit and in truth" (Jn. 4:23-24).

"When the history of salvation has further progressed, it will be
seen that the temple was superfluous to this history," though Jesus agrees
that God's revelation was safeguarded in Judaism, and not in the
Samaritan aberration from it.[11] May one not say, too, that as the spiritual
history of the individual also progresses, temple worship may become
superfluous? We are so used to it, and both training and tradition have
dinned it into us that *Puja* and the *Sanskaras,* Church-going and the
Sacraments are necessary characteristic of a religious person, that we
often tend to confuse "religious" and "spiritual". Many people who
are "religious" — devout temple or church goers, offerers of *Pujaa*
and *Yagna* — may not be truly "spiritual" at all; and contrariwise,
among many post-Christians — as in the West — and increasingly among
youths in some parts of India — there are sincere "spiritual" people,
seeking God and worshipping Him "in spirit and in truth," whom one
may ignorantly condemn or pity as irreligious.

7. "God is spirit"

Paul speaks of Him as "life-giving spirit" (1 Cor. 15:45). Spirit,
in the biblical sense, describes God's life-giving activity rather than
defines his nature (cf. 1:32). God is spirit in that He gives the Spirit,
as God is light and love (1 Jn. 1:5; 4:8, etc.). This explains how and

why the true worshipper of God must worship Him in Spirit and Truth. The two words actually signify a single idea.

Again, we may get new insight on this from the word in other scriptures. Thus, Chandogya Upanishad, speaking of *Atman*, the pure spirit — beyond sorrow, old age and death, beyond evil, hunger, and thirst, says: "It is Atman, whose love is Truth, whose thoughts are truth" (Ch. Up. 8.1) and again: "This is Atman, the Spirit in man. All the desires of this Spirit are truth. It is this Spirit that we must find and know: man must find his own self. He who has found, and knows His Self, has found all the worlds, has achieved all is desires." Thus spoke Prajapati.

After living with him for years to seek this Spirit, Indra and Virochan were told, "What you see when you look into another person's eyes, that is Atman, immortal, beyond fear, that is Brahman."

"And who is he whom we see when we look in water or in a mirror?" they asked.

"The same is seen in all," he answered. And then he said to them: "Go and look at yourselves in a bowl of water and ask me anything you want to know about the Atman, your own self! By thus looking at themselves they learned that they were not their bodies, and — after more years of thought and living with the Guru, discovered that the body , too, is 'the house of the Spirit'; that if a man is ruled by his body, then this man can never be free. But when a man is in the joy of the Spirit, in the Spirit which is ever free, then this man is free from all bondage" (cf. Chand Up. 8.7-12).

It was this fredom of the Spirit that Jesus came essentially to give; the "living waters" meant the Spirit who is joy, *Anandam*, and which, like love, casts out fear. "For he who sees all beings in his own self and his own self in all beings, loses all fear" (Isa. Up. 6). The more one learns to find Him within oneself, the more easily one sees Him in others. The same Self is seen in another person's eyes as in one's own heart; seated in the heart of all things. This throws light, too, on the commandment "Love your neighbor as yourself." It is the Spirit in one who loves in us; it is He who prays in us. "God has sent forth the Spirit of his son into our hearts, crying 'Abba, Father' (Gal. 4:6). The man who realizes the Atman, knowing 'I am He,' what craving or what urge could cause him to cling to the body?" (Brihad Up. IV 4.12).

8. "I am He"

"I who am speaking to you, I am He," said Jesus (v. 26) to the woman, when she tried to tell Him that when the Messiah came, he would tell them all things. She had surmised that He was perhaps the Prophet of Deuteronomy 18:18. ("I will raise up a prophet like yourself for them from their own brothers. I will put my words into his mouth and he shall tell them all I command him.")[12] Again Christ breaks through her smoke screen and brooks no compromise. "Only one thing is necessary — knowing me, and thus the Father. But that is the gift of the Spirit." This is what — to all intents and purposes — Jesus tells her. "I who am speaking to you — *I am*" reproduces Yahweh's pronouncement of Is. 52:6. "My people know my name; that day they will understand that it is I who say 'I am here.' " In view of the special significance of "I am" as Jesus' designation of Himself in John, it is likely that John characteristically suggests another level of meaning here in Jesus' affirmation.[13] This is one of Jesus' "I am" formulae without a predicate — like *Aham asmi*. The "I am" formula without a predicate is characteristic of the language of the Johananine Christ.[14] The name of Yahweh Himself (Ex. 3:14), considered blasphemous for anyone to use, is used by John to show the nature and mission of the Word incarnate, the Son of God. And yet, are we not all to be "sons in the Son"? This means we have all to learn to become and remain aware of this "I," this "Self" in us — which grows in proportion as the *ahamkar* (ego) or self (with a small 's') dies — until we can all say with St. Paul: "I live, now, not I, but Christ lives in me" or with Tukaram, "The I within me now is dead and Thou enthroned instead, Yes, this I, Tuka, testify. . .no longer now is 'me' or 'my.' "

Ramana Maharishi, who taught his disciples to inquire constantly, "Who am I?" said, "Other thoughts might come and go like the various notes of music, but the 'I' continues with all other notes. Remain aware of the 'I.' This awareness is the water turning into a spring inside him, welling up to eternal life."

Jesus' "I am He" to the Samaritan woman is the climax, as it were, of this beautiful and very human encounter by the well of Jacob. At this point in the story, Jesus' disciples returned from their marketing and "were surprised to find him speaking to a woman" (v. 27). They are not yet used to His spirit — the spirit of freedom. In the meantime, the woman, forgetting all about her water pot, and all that it stood for, ran off and told the people around, "Come and see a man who has told me everything I ever did; could he be the Christ?" People impressed by her testimony walked towards Jesus. They in turn fell under his spell and "begged him to stay with them" (v. 40).

9. Sharing the waters

It is interesting to see how immediately the woman, having drunk of the "living water" from the heart of Christ, herself becomes an apostle — like that other woman, Magdalen, who was the first apostle of the Risen Lord. The "living water" already becomes a "spring within" her and begins to flow out to others. In Jyoti Sahi's inspiring painting of this scene of the Gospel, the woman is seen — almost on her toes, being drawn up and into his heart, as it were, from where she yearningly "draws" the living water, and simultaneously she herself becomes a living stream of that great gushing water. Jyoti explains his painting: "Water flows from what in Hindu terms might be called 'the cave' of Christ's heart. The woman at the well becomes part of that stream, in that she herself seems to impersonate the feminine force of nature which is here spoken of as having its true source in Christ. In Indian art the spirits of rivers and wells are often personified in the forms of woman" (cf. Ganga-mata). "Christ is shown in this picture as seated in meditation, the stream of life flowing from the 'cave of his heart.' "[16]
It is significant, too, and bears special meaning for India, that in this picture Christ is depicted as sitting by the well in *padmasan* — the Lotus posture — in meditation. It is those who spend time in "just sitting," as the Soto Zen Buddhist meditators would say, who can really pass on life-giving waters to others. Often, on the contrary, they are taken as wasters and idlers, yet they are the real life-savers and life-givers. Those monks, *sannyasis*, contemplatives, "live at the very Source." It is not that they are self-centered egoists unconcerned about the true interests of the world. Quite the contrary. "The *Sadhu's* self is supposed to have expanded to the limits of the universe, to share the

very infinity of the Self. He lives at the very source. . .and his work, if one may put it so, is to make sure that the water flows plentifully and unceasingly from the source itself to the water-works and canals further downstream which are not his concern. There are others whose duty is to see to them.''[17] Thus Christ sitting by the well, apparently doing nothing — while his active disciples went to the town to buy food (v. 8) — is really waiting for the thirsting woman — to give her the true waters of life.

10. "Saviour of the world"

When many Samaritans, impressed by His Spirit, came to believe in Him, they say to the woman (as though they were anxious to remind her that she was but a woman and should not think too much of herself as the cause of their faith in Him!), "Now we no longer believe because of what you told us; we have heard Him ourselves and we know that He really is the Saviour of the world" (v. 42), not merely "King of Israel" (Jn. 1:49). This world perspective is typical of John. He is the Saviour of all — offering life-giving waters to all men and women, high and low, rich and poor, intelligent and stupid alike, and leading all to worship the Father, as though in answer to a Rig Vedic prayer of old:

> Be Thou our Saviour, show Thyself our own, Looking after and showing mercy to the worshippers; Friend, Father, Fatherliest of fathers Giving to the living worshipper free space and life. (Rig. veda iv 17.17).

In the Rig Veda it was asked: "Who is the deity we shall adore with our oblation?" (x. 121). Jesus here shows that it is not the deity "in Jerusalem or on this mountain" but He who lives in the cave of the heart (who is the Self of all things) and who seeks to be worshipped "in spirit and in truth." Only thus the worshipper gets "free space and life." Both gifts asked for are typical of the Vedas. *Lokam* is the wide world whose saviour He is! *Kyah* is life which He said He had come to give (Jn. 10:10). The life-force is symbolized by the waters of the river that flows from his heart.

In a Hindi hymn we sing: *Jeevan-Jal, Jeevan-jal, he Prabho mujhe de. Tere Hridayme-se Gangaji jo bahti hai, vah mujhe de.*

(Lord, give me the waters of life, the living waters, the waters of the Ganges that flow from out your heart.)

CHAPTER FIVE

Healing Waters

John 5:1-15

Water had been used as an instrument by Jesus for his first miracle at Cana, changing water into wine (Jn. 2:1-12). Now he uses it for another "sign", healing a paralytic of thirty-eight years standing. The waters of a well had been the locale for a woman being introduced to the mystery of "living waters" which Christ came to offer (Jn. 4:1-42). Now the waters of a pool are to be used to show the power of Jesus — his life-giving power, which, as he claimed in the discourse that followed this miracle, he shared with the Father; to show, too, how his power of curing was greater than and independent of the natural elements. Was he not the master of all created elements, as he would show Peter by walking on water?

1. At the pool of Bethzatha

Jesus went up to Jerusalem for a feast. John does not identify the "Jewish festival" — possibly Pentecost or Tabernacles. Its importance is secondary to what took place at the time. He does, however, especially mention the place — the Sheep-pool in Jerusalem called Bethzatha (Bethesda means "house of mercy"), consisting of five porticos. The name was given to a building erected by a pool whose waters were said to have curative effects. But the name really had quite a different meaning. Its Semitic form has been recovered in the copper scroll of Qumuan Cave III — *bet'esdatayin* — "house of the double gusher," a name that referred to the springs that fed the double pool. John's purpose in giving the Hebrew name is to qualify the pool as "water of Judaism," as in John 2:6, "the six stone water jars" for Jewish ablutions are specified, and in John 4:12 the well of Jacob, where Jesus met the Samaritan woman.[1] The Sheep-pool has been identified with the double-pool that now lies near the Church of St. Anne in Jerusalem. I remember sitting by it some years ago, meditating on the cure of the paralytic on this spot. How vividly one could imagine the whole scene; the waters suddenly stirring and gushing, and almost instantly a huge scramble among those lying in the porticos who had been waiting long and nervously for this precise moment, each hoping his friends and loved ones would somehow manage to get him down into the waters to be the first, so as to be cured. For under the porticos lay "crowds of sick people — blind, lame, paralyzed, waiting for the water to move, for at intervals, the angel of the Lord came down into the pool and the water was disturbed, and the first person to enter the water after this disturbance was cured of any ailment he suffered from" (Jn. 5:3-4). It was probably an inflow of fresh water from time to time that disturbed the pond. According to some scholars, part of these verses (3b and 4) are missing in the oldest manuscript (including P 66 and P 75) and the language is not Johannine. There can be hardly any doubt that we have in them a later edition devised to explain (v. 7).[2]

2. "Waters stored with healing balm"

Lourdes (Fatima), Ganga, St. Winifred's Well in England! One can think of several such "holy" places where the waters of pools, lakes, ponds, streams or rivers attract crowds, for they are known as healing waters which can cure men of physical and, sometimes, more miraculously perhaps, though less manifestly and spectacularly, spiritual ailments. The waters are instrumental in curing bodies and souls — as though in answer to an ancient prayer: "Loose the bonds of sin that bind me!"

God made the rivers to flow. They feel no weariness, they cease not from flowing. They fly swiftly like birds in the air. May the stream of my life flow into the river of righteousness.

> Loose the bonds of sin that bind me.
>
> > Rig Ved 11-28
>
> You Waters who rule over precious things and have supreme control of men,
> We beg you, give us healing balm.
> Within the waters, Soma has told me, remedies exist of every sort.
> O Waters stored with healing balm, through which my body safe will be,
> Come that I long may see the sun.
> Whatever sin is found in me, whatever wrong I may have done,
> Waters, remove it far from me.
>
> > Rig Ved X.9.5-8

The importance of hydropathy recognized by us only in recent times was well known in Vedic times. The healing power of water is sung also in Rig Ved VI.50.7:

> Waters! friends of men! In peace and in trouble.
> Give your blessings to your sons and grandsons.
> For you are the most motherly physicians,
> the mother of all that stands and all that moves.

The medicative and curative powers of water are also referred to in Atharva Ved. I.6.2:

> Within the waters, Soma has told me,
> Are all medicines that heal —
> The waters contain all medicines.

Remedies of every sort exist in the waters for all sorts of diseases. So it was believed in Israel too. This man was paralyzed and though the Gospel does not say that he had spent all his thirty-eight years at the pool (v.7), it presupposes that he had been there a long time. Was he perhaps a representative of the Israelites who had wandered and waited for thirty-eight years for the fulfillment of God's promise?

3. Divine courtesy and caring

Jesus saw him lying there among the crowds. He knew his plight and that he had been lying there for years — each time his hope frustrated but never completely quenched in his heart. Here is one of the "signs" where Jesus Himself first approaches the man to be cured without being asked. He asks the Man: "Do you want to be well again?" Divine courtesy respects man's free will with superlative delicacy! Nor will God touch man without his consent and desire — waiting patiently for his cloud of *avidya* to pass till he sees the light of the sun enough to want to have his heart changed. For it is always for a change of heart — conversion — that Jesus cures a physical ailment. What would it profit a man if he had a healthy body and suffered the loss of his higher Self? When the man complains that someone else always manages to go down before him into the healing waters and therefore he cannot be cured, Jesus sees beyond his words, a desire to be healed. He proceeds to show him that he can cure him independently of the waters that heal or their movement. Was it not this spirit that "moved over the waters" at the beginning of the world? "Get up," he said to the man, "pick up your sleeping mat and walk" — Immediately the man got well; he picked up his mat and started walking" (v. 8-9). The man no doubt had not expected this. His vision was limited; he thought perhaps that Jesus would extend to him the kindness of helping him in — and this time he would be the first to get into the pool and thus be cured. His mind had been conditioned for years that there was only one way he could ever be cured, i.e., through the instrumentality of the waters. He may have believed simply that it was "an angel of the Lord" who came down at the intervals in the pool to cure. He may not have known that whenever the water bubbled, when the intermittent underground spring that fed the pool became more active, it was thought to be especially curative. Doubtless this condition would last only for a short while so that those in charge of the building would surely have been forced to regulate the crowds, possiby allowing only one person to enter the water. Or it may have been thought that the water was then effective only for one person.[3] However that may be and whatever the man thought, Jesus did with one word what the water or anyone else had been unable to do for him. Without referring to the curative value of the water, He competely healed his infirmity.

4. Jesus' fondness of water for healing

And yet somehow Jesus seems to have linked and gradually caused to transfer the man's faith in the healing waters to faith in Himself. He undoubtedly seemed fond of linking water's curative powers with Himself — using them as His instruments of healing. It is as though Jesus were the fulfillment of yet another scriptural deity, not only of Indian mythology, but going back to the Indo-Iranian period. The *Apam Napat* of the Rig Veda (II.35.9) "represents what amounts to an invariant in all ancient cultures of mankind."[4] He, the Spirit of the waters, is "the Son of the Waters, of color unfading, performing his works within the body of another" (Rig Veda II.35.13). Agni is "the son of the waters," dwelling in the waters. There are innumerable places in Rig Veda I where Agni's connection with the waters is mentioned. Fire and water belong together. In later Christian art one sees Jesus showing his heart on fire — aflame with love. One could "fantasize," think of Christ as the true son of waters, the Lord who, by the greatness of divine dominion, has created all beings, the pure, the Shining Son of Waters (Rig Vida ii.35.2). For *Apam Napat* is brilliant and and youthful; he shines without fuel in the waters which surround and nourish him. Clothed in lightning, he is golden in form and appearance. Standing in the highest place, he always shines with undimmed splendor. In the Avesta, *Apam Napat* is a spirit of the waters who lives in their depths, who is said to have seized the brightness in the depth of the ocean.[5]

Jesus is "the Shining Son of Waters," who cures men of all kinds of diseases with the power of the flame that burns in his heart — using water in various forms and ways.

Thus we see a paralled case of a disabled man born blind in John 9. Jesus spat on the ground and made some mud with the spittle; he rubbed the mud on the man's eyes and said: "Go and wash your face in the pool of Siloam." (This name means "sent.") So the man went, washed his face and came back seeing (v. 6-7). In the blind man's case Jesus first uses his spittle (as also in Mk. 7:33 and 8:23). Spittle was commonly believed to have medicinal properties. Spittle is yet another form of water. Jesus, always respectfully mindful of the common usages and practices of the times and place in which he was incarnated, uses it for curing people.

Interestingly enough for us, it was to a pool that he sent the blind man to wash — though he could have cured his sight only through his spittle. Perhaps it was because the water drawn from that pool during the feast of tabernacles symbolized the blessings of the Messianic age. Henceforth he showed that the source of these blessings would be Jesus Himself; so he "sent" him to the pool of Siloe. "The Envoy" or "The One Sent" is one of John's favorite names for Christ (cf. Jn. 3:17, 34; 5:36).

5. Nothing to do with past sin

It is interesting and important, too, to note that on both these occasions of cure, Jesus makes it clear that the sick men's sins were not responsible for their affliction. When his disciples asked "Rabbi, who sinned? This man or his parents, for him to have been born blind?" Jesus showed that his blindness had nothing to do with the past "karma" — neither his nor his parents, but "so that God's power might be seen at work in him" (v. 3). When he finds the paralytic again in the temple, he warns him: "Stop sinning or something worse may happen to you" (5:14). He does not say his paralysis was the result of sin but that his cure was a divine favor that must be acknowledged by conversion of life (cf. Jn. 9:2-8, Luke 13:1-4). To forget this is to risk something worse than the disease.

6. Jesus puts the Spirit before the law

When the man picked up his sleeping mat and started walking, the Jewish authorities told him it was wrong to carry the mat on that day, for the cure took place on a Sabbath. The healed man answered that he who had cured him told him to do so. But when asked, "Who is the man who told you to do this?" he could not tell; for Jesus had slipped away in the crowd (v. 10-12). Now these verses tell us a great deal about Jesus. Not only had He shown that He had power over life and health — independent of "the moving of the waters," and that he cared for man's total liberation, eager to remove pain, but now he also showed his utter disdain of the law, if it meant putting the law before the Spirit. He had shown elsewhere that the Sabbath is made for man, not man for the Sabbath. For Jesus it was the Spirit that always mattered most.

7. Unassuming simplicity

Another important and beautiful characteristic of Jesus that comes out of this story is His not wanting to take any credit for Himself. The man had no idea who had cured him — so fast had Jesus slipped away among the crowds. Like the very waters that flow from the Source — without passing to claim acknowledgment or gratitude from those they had healed, washed, given to drink — so he had passed on to his Source — the Father, concerned only with fulfilling his will — to do "the works my Father has given me to carry out" (v. 36) as he said in the discourse that followed this miracle, though he knew well and claimed that as the Father raises the dead and gives them life, so the Son gives life to anyone he chooses (v. 21; cf. Matt. 11:25, Jn. 11:42).

8. Freedom from human respect

Jesus was sovereignly free from seeking man's honor and approval. Therefore he could afford to reproach them for "seeking honor one from another instead of the approval that comes from God alone" (cf. v. 44). "As for human approval," he said, "this means nothing to me" (v. 41). Like the waters that flow on fully free, he went on doing his Father's will — irrespective of men's reactions. And, in fact, he pointed to this human respect from which all men suffer, as one of the main blocks to their receiving him in faith. "You like to receive praise from one another but you do not try to win praise from the One who alone is God; how then can you believe me?" (v. 44). How very often we are blocked from seeing as God sees, through our fear of men's opinions of us! How utterly free Jesus is, for "He knew what was in man," and did not trust Himself to them (Jn. 2:25). He knew how very unreliable man was, yet loved Him with compassion and "unto the end" (13:1). Even when the Pharisees thought "the whole world is running after Him" (Jn. 12:19), Jesus knew the same hearts that had been fascinated by Him would soon be plotting His death. He knew that even among the leading men who did believe in Him, there was hesitation to acknolwedge Him; they did not admit it through fear of the Pharisees and fear of being expelled from the synagogue: they put honor from men before the honor that comes from God (Jn. 12.42.43). And yet He who claimed that He did "only what He saw the Father doing" (Jn. 5:19) and spoke only "what the Father has told me" (Jn. 12:50) was not believed. Man had "never heard His voice and never seen His shape" — for God is beyond all *nam* and *roop* (name and form). And yet when He took name and form and came "that you may have life" (Jn. 10:10), man refused to believe. "His word finds no home in you because you do not believe in the one He has sent" (v. 38). And not to believe is not to have life.

9. "You refuse to come to me" (Jn 5:40)

One of the most startling sayings of Jesus regarding faith in Him — on which He consistently insisted — comes in the discourse with the Jews that followed the cure of this man at the pool. To "come to" Jesus means to have faith in Him. "Whoever listens to my words and believes in the one who sent me, has eternal life [note: not "will have"]; without being brought to judgment he has passed [already!] from death to life" (v. 24). The pleading prayer of our Vedantic ancestors hundreds of years before Christ, and which is still repeated daily by thousands of our Hindu brothers, *Mrtyor ma amrtam gamaya* (from death lead me to life), has been not just promised, but already fufilled — for him

who believes that "the Father who is the Source of life has made the
Son the source of life" (v. 26). Jesus was to say later to the cured man
when He found him in the temple, "Beware lest something worse may
happen to you" (Jn. 5:;14). What "worse thing" can happen to the
man that Jesus warns him about? It would be "not to pass from death
to life." This was the point of the miracle and of the discourse. In John,
a miracle and the discourse that follows are fundamentally one,[6] and
to me, this is one of Jesus' finest discourses. This is the great lesson
He tried to bring home to the Jews by working the cure of the man
at the pool of Probatica. But because their hearts were too involved
and entangled in what others thought or would think of them, they dared
not give their faith or allegiance to Jesus and thus they chose death rather
than to "come to me for life" (v. 40). One can almost palpably feel
the pain, the disappointment, the yearning and compassion of the heart
of Christ — in these words of John, John who had leaned "on His breast"
and listened to the beat of His heart!

10. "The gift of God Most High"

The way in which John has arranged the following verses of Jesus'
discourse indicates that he did not attempt to report any specific
conversation but that instead he has summarized what was brought out
on the subject of his attitude to the Sabbath obligation, in various
controversies.[7] I have already referred to parts of this discourse. It is
divided into two parts: a) the life-giving power of the Father and the
Son (v. 19-30), which is illustrated by the miracle at the pool; b) the
witness which the Father bears to the Son (v. 31-47) besides the witness
of John and the witness of Jesus' works. Among many soul-stirring
words of Jesus in this discourse there are two particularly significant
and lovely words that I like to ponder on — in the light of the Upanishads
— v. 21 and v. 39: "The Son gives life to anyone he chooses" (v. 21)
and "You study the Scriptures believing that in them you have eternal
life" (v. 39).

"To anyone he chooses" reminds one of Matthew 11:27, which
has a distinctly Johannine flavor: "No one knows the Father except

the Son and those to whom the Son chooses to reveal Him." The attainment of God realization is essentially a grace. *Mokshamulam Guru-Kripa* (The grace of the Guru-or-God is the root of salvation) as is sung in the Guru-Gita. And yet Sri Ramana Maharishi and other Vedantins would say that there is no question of grace except from the point of view of one who still sees duality. It is the Self — the Atman — who alone freely reveals itself — shining with its own light.

"The Atman is beyond sound and form, without touch and taste and perfume — indeed, above reasoning. When consciousness of the Atman manifests itself, man becomes free from the jaws of death" (Katha Up. 3.15). "The Self cannot be gained by the Veda nor by understanding, nor by much learning; he whom the Self chooses, by him the Self can be gained. To him the Self reveals his own form" (Katha Up. II.2.23). "It is only those who are given to me by the Father who came to me, whom I keep," Jesus will repeat (Jn. 6:37; 10:20 f.). In the last analysis all is gift. "The Christian knows that everything that the Upanishad attributes to man has been received by him as a free gift and uncovenanted grace. He exists, but in God, and through the gift of God which is the Spirit. . .all that he is, he is in the communication of the Spirit."[8]

No mere human effort, however strenuous, not even the study of Scriptures, can attain God. Only he can attain to Him in whom the Spirit gives witness by "manifesting" itself from within. This point is well put in John 5:9-10: "If we receive the testimony of men, the testimony of God is greater; for this is the testimony of God that He has borne witness to his Son. He who believes in the Son of God has the testimony in himself."

This is the direct witness of the Father to men; what Calvin in a later age called "the internal testimony of the Holy Spirit." Paul put it in his own way: "No one can say 'Jesus is Lord' except by the Holy Spirit" (1 Cor. 12:3). "The Father has borne witness in the hearts of those who have believed in the Son, but this does not include the Jews, because the Jews will not believe."[9] And God had "chosen" them to be especially His people, yet have we not all within us something of the spirit of the non-believing Jew? Perhaps precisely because we "seek honor one from another and the honor that comes form God alone we do not seek" (5:44)!

11. Faith in the Word and self-awakening

They thought they would find God by searching the Scriptures. "You search the Scriptures," said Jesus. "It is they that bear witness to me." The verb "search" here can be either indicative or imperative. Marsh, among others, thinks that the indicative gives by far the better sense, and suggests that we read for "and" — "and yet."[10] True enough, "the same Scriptures" speak of him. "It was I that he [Moses] was writing about, but if you refuse to believe what he wrote, how can you believe what I say?" (5:47). It is their lack of faith that Jesus blames. yet an attitude of faith is a *sine qua non* to the Final Awakening.

It is significant that the understanding of the secrets of the Vedanta (the Upanishads) demand not an initiation rite — as do the Vedas — but an interior attitude of faith on the part of the student; an openness to the mystery, trusting without doubt both the Guru's word and the word of Scripture, yet always pressing on beyond them. "It is a faith whose inner flame will be kindled by a deep experience, by the discovery — still obscure and inarticulate — of the secret it reveals." For the Upanishads, as Swami Abhishiktananda points out, do not consist primarily of revealed truths which can be transmitted through the medium of concepts and words, even if one has to admit that all passing on of experience has to be done, at least in the early stages, in this way.[11] The student of the Bible, it may be true to say in general, is too much bound by and restricted to words and concepts. Perhaps it is because though the Bible is an Asian product, most of its scholars and commentators, its teachers and even meditators, have so far been brought up on the Western approach to exegisis, hermeneutics, theologizing, and even praying — constantly stressing more perhaps than anything else, the revealed truths. Whereas the Upanishads do not consist primarily of revealed truths which the *rishis* (seers) could transmit through the medium of concepts and words, even if one has to use the latter, at least in the first stages of the seeker's spiritual search and evolution. The Upanishadic seer is much less the man who "knows this or that" than the man who "knows thus," *evam*, as the Upanishads constantly reiterate, calling him *evamvid* (one who knows thus). It is a way of perceiving everything differently; it is not new information but much more an awakening to the self within, to an unsuspected death in oneself and therefore to the mystery of all things and to THE Mystery — God. The Upanishads can only be communicated in "the cave of the heart." "The only possible alternative to the Guru's instruction is an openness of oneself to the inner mystery so complete, that it allows the true sense of the scriptures to be discerned beyond the words, the parables and the paradoxes."[12]

12. The Scriptures converge on Jesus — their focus[13]

Might not one say that Our Lord is the center of all Scriptures, not only the Old and New Testaments? Yet it is not the Scriptures themselves but the Spirit of Self within man — the same Spirit who is the author of the Scriptures — who can make man attain to God. This communication of the word of Scripture can only be done by the Guru who is so without self that he can communicate the Self. He is so "capable of being at home in the very heart of the disciple and so of opening the disciple to his own self — of awakening him to himself within the Guru's own self-awakening."[14] In this sense Jesus is the Satguru. He was able to do precisely this to the man at the pool. But this presupposes in the disciple a total faith, as we have seen. Only so can the true sense of the Scriptures be discerned and understood. How often in the Gospels one reads of Jesus being disappoitned, surprised, almost exasperated by his disciples' lack of understanding, lack of faith? "Do you not yet understand? Do you not perceive? O ye of little faith!"

13. The source of healing waters

Jesus was to say clearly, "He who has seen me has seen the Father" (Jn. 14:9). The man paralyzed for thirty-eight years and who patiently waited to be liberated did not at his first encounter with Christ recognize him to be his liberator. He was looking for his salvation to come from the waters of the pool. When he met Jesus a second time, that was a real *darshan* of the Father for him; a manifestation of God which made him realize that once he was bereft of human respect and fear, he could be touched and healed by God and awakened to the Self within.

He now understood that the miracle was meant to be but a "sign" of his spiritual resurrection. His spirit of faith and discipleship was awakened to the mystery of Realization. He was now able to go beyond the signs and Sabbath rules of picking up or not picking up mats. He had "listened" and "believed in the One who sent" Jesus (Jn. 5:24), and therefore had passed through not the waters of the pool but the waters of death to the "further shore" of life. He had seen and understood that the man who cured him was the Source "whence all healing waters flow."

CHAPTER SIX

Walking on the Waters

John 6:16-21

The crowds by the Sea of Galilee or Tiberius had been enthused at seeing Jesus' miracle of the multiplication of loaves, feeding five thousand with five loaves and two fishes and having twelve baskets of pieces left over (Jn. 6:1-13). Seeing this miracle, the people said, "Surely this is the Prophet who was to come into the world!" But Jesus, knowing that they wanted to seize him in order to make him king by force, went off again to the hills by himself (v. 14-15).

1. The Sea of Galilee

"The Sea of Galilee" is the ordinary New Testament designation of the Galilean lake called in the Old Testament the Sea of Chinnerath (Num. 34:11). "Or Lake Tiberias" it is thought was added by John or someone else later (cf. 21:1) for precision and updating. Tiberias, a city on the western shore, was founded by Herod Antipas sometime after A.D. 20 and named for the Emperor Tiberius, and subsequenlty gave its name to the lake.[1] Jesus, during his public life, was often seen going across this lake or sea, sitting and preaching on its shores, or from a boat on the lake, and one may be sure there were innumerable other occasions, not recorded in the Gospels, when Jesus looked at and loved those beautifully blue waters. I think it is one of the loveliest spots I have seen hallowed by the Lord's presence in the Holy Land. We have seen Jesus with the Baptist by a river, the Jordan. We have met him with the Samaritan woman by a well, the well of Jacob. We have witnessed His healing the paralytic by a pool — the pool of Probatica. We now have His *darshan* on the waters of a lake or the sea of Galilee. Knowing the illusory enthusiasm of the people, which probably his disciples also shared, Jesus rejects their attempts to "make him king" as emphatically as he had rejected Satan's temptations, in the wilderness (Lk. 4:1-13; Matt. 4:1-11). How unlike most of us, who would have loved to have been honored and esteemed. "He fled back to the mountain alone" (v. 15) and then "forced" the disciples to cross the Lake of Galilee again immediately after the miracle of the loaves. "When evening came, Jesus' disciples went down to the lake, got into a boat and went back across the lake towards Capernaum. Night came on and Jesus still had not come to them" (v. 16-17).

2. The fifth sign

Now Jesus works his fifth "sign." Though the bulk of the chapter (Jn. 6) dealt with bread, water is not missing and, as with the miracle of the loaves, the significance of the "sign" will appear only later (v. 68), as we shall see. "Night came on and Jesus still had not come." And to add to the darkness and being without Jesus, a third obstacle presents itself — as in life so often. A strong wind began to blow and to stir up the water (v. 18). This was a common occurrence on a lake subject to sudden storms. John describes it quite simply and naturally. He does not make much of the storm, whereas the Synoptics, writing of the same incident, show Jesus' power not only over the waves, by walking on them, but also in quieting the powerful wind (Mk. 6:51; Matt. 14-32). But John is concerned — like us — more with Jesus' power over the waters. His purpose was not that of the Synoptics.

3. Within the heart is sufficiency

"They saw Jesus walking on the waters, coming near the boat (v. 19). When the night is dark and Jesus seems absent, sometimes He suddenly appears — in unexpected ways; sometimes He makes us wait; showing His sovereign freedom and infinite power, but above all, His concern for man. He had already shown that He did not need to rely on "the moving waters of the pond to heal the paralytic. Now he shows himself walking steadily on those moving waters, as though it were as easy and natural to walk on them as on the *terra firma*. And so it was for Him. For not only was He the Lord and Master of water as of earth; all His power came from within, not from outside Himself. It was the same mysterious power of the living water which Christ gave the Samaritan woman. "He who draws at the font finds a fountain with Himself" (Jn. 4:14). The same power within His heart he could transfer into man's — the same "living water" of the Spirit. All his resources were within Himself; were Himself (as He was to show so majestically later by the momentous words "It is I" (v. 20). He came to teach us in turn to find the same resources within our own hearts. Ramana Maharishi was right in insisting so much on the importance of meditating "on Thee in the heart."

> O Sun, whose bright rays swallow up the whole world,
> May your grace make my heart-lotus blossom.
>
> Mar Garland v. 27

The point of this story is — and this is what concerns John — that in the "heart-lotus" of Christ is sole sufficiency; that He himself and He alone can satisfy man's hunger as men and slake men's real thirst. For the sake of man He even goes to the extent of asking for a drink — not only when sitting tired by a well (Jn. 4:7), but even when suffering acute thirst, hanging like a criminal on the cross (Jn. 19:28). Yet all the oceans of waters were His. He could give them or walk on them as easily as He had created them.

4. "Coming towards the boat"

Water is used here for Jesus to "come towards" the boat — as though He could not wait till they reached the shore. If man thirsts for God, God's thirst for man is still greater. And yet, often, such is the mystery of His love that He does not hasten "to come towards" our sinking boat. He waits and makes us wait — as though to heighten our desire for Him, to deepen our thirst and trust still more. He makes us row on , conscious though He is of the gale sweeping down upon us and the rough waters threatening to drown us. He waits — standing on the shore, as He was to do at a later date in His disciples' training (Jn. 21:4). As Simone Weil once said, expectation in patient waiting is the foundation of spiritual life. Padavano agrees with this. "An understanding of Jesus begins with a theology of patient expectation. Jesus must be awaited. He is not sudden. He comes to patient hearts; to those willing to be alone as they wait."[2] And thus he chose to sit by the well and wait for the woman with five husbands (Jn. 4). Here he chooses to wait for his moment and then go forward — walking on the sea, to allay the fears of His disciples in the boat.

Or did He just wait on the shore and make them wait — and never go forward?

Some commentators think that the original Greek means not "on the sea" but "by the sea," and that in the stormy, overcast condition the disciples thought He was in the middle of the lake when He was really on the shore.[3] That is why they maintain that the words "immediately the boat was at land" or "in the place they were heading for" — (Good News Bible translation, v. 21) which is considered by some as a "miracle within a miracle" was merely natural; for Jesus was already near the land.

Others, however, think that John, like the Synoptics, is showing the power attributed to Yahweh in the Old Testament of having "his way through the sea," his "path through the waters," although "his footprints were not seen" (cf. Ps. 77:19). In short, they are making basically theological statements about the person of Jesus. The point John is making here, then, is that whether Jesus waits or walks towards us on water, both are equally easy for Him, for His power is within

Himself. And Wijngaards, speaking of the seven signs chosen by John, says: "Walking on water shows Jesus to be the only true guide, as turning water into wine showed him bringing newness of life."[4]

5. And they were terrified (Jn. 6:19)

Whether Jesus walks on the waters towards our boat or waits for us on the shore, what He is telling us is that God has power over the sea — whose waters can at times be frightening. It is a commonplace theme in the Old Testament (Gen. 2:11, 6 f; Ps. 74:12-15; 93:3 f., etc.). More especially it was through his control of the sea that the first Israel had emerged in the Exodus (Ex. 14:19 f.; 15:1-21; Ps. 77:17-21). Just as the miracle of the loaves portrayed Jesus as a new Moses, so Jesus will be brought out in the following discourse as one greater than Moses. The present miracle underlines the power of Him who was to bring forth the new Israel.[5] We can see reflected in Jesus' authority Yahweh's power (Ps. 107:23-32) and his "wonderful works." It is God who enables us to "cross the waters" — whether like the Israelites crossing the Red Sea or as in the Rig Vedic poem which says:

> The river full of stones flows on;
> Move together my comrades!
> Stand erect and cross it!
> Let us leave here those that are evil
> We will cross over to the powers of goodness.
>
> Rig Ved. X.53.8

The disciples were understandably frightened both by the storm and perhaps even more by seeing Jesus walking on the waters towards them. Waters which can slake thirst, cleanse, heal, soothe, give indescribable joy and satisfaction, can also at times be terrifying. Water is not merely a power of life. Waters from the sea can reflect demoniacal restlessness by their perpetual agitation, and the desolation of Sheol by their bitterness. The sudden swelling of the west wind blowing away the earth and living things during a storm (Job 12:15; 40:23) symbolizes the misfortune that is prepared to fall upon man unexpectedly (Ps. 124) or the plots that the just man's enemies weave against him (Ps. 18:5f, 17; 42:8; 71:20; 144:7). Now if God knows how to protect the just man from these destructive tides (Ps. 32:6), He can just as easily permit them to break over the godless (cf. Job 22:11). For the prophets of the Old Testament, the destructive overflowing of the great rivers symbolizes the power of the kingdoms that go to submerge and destroy small nations; the power of Assyria compared to the river Euphrates (Is. 8:7) or of Egypt likened to the waters of the Nile (Jer. 46:7 f.). These rivers symbolize God's punishment of people who fail to trust in Him (Is. 8:6 f.).

In the hands of God, whose heart is all love, this brutal scourge is never blind. Though it swallows up the godless world (2 Pet. 2-5) the flood allows His lovers or those who trust in Him, like Noah the just man, to survive (Wis. 10:18 f.). The terrifying waters then anticipate the final judgment by fire (2 Pet. 2-5), the flood allows His lovers or those who trust in Him — like Noah the just man — to survive (Wis. 10.18 f.). The terrifying waters then anticipate the final judgment by fire (2 Pet. 3:5 f.), but they have a new earth after their passage (Gen. 8:11).[6] That is why, however terrifying the waters of life, God walks on them towards us and give us the assurance of a new promise of hope.

6. "Do not be afraid" (Jn. 6:20)

Man's quailing heart constantly needs this assurance. Fear can be more terrifying and paralyzing than raging waters. We all know it experientially — not only by reading in the Gospels of the disciples' cowardice or failure to stand by Jesus, their failure to trust Him. Man with his fearful heart needs to put his trust in someone. According to where he puts his trust, "he is cursed or blessed." The man who trusts in man is cursed "like a shrub in the desert. . .he shall dwell in the parched places of the wilderness. Blessed is the man who trusts in the Lord, whose trust is the Lord" (the "I am" — Him who "is"). For "he is like a tree planted by water that sends out roots by the stream and does not fear when the heat comes, for its leaves remain green and it is not anxious in the year of drought; for it does not cease to bear fruit" (Jer. 17:6-8). Jesus constantly calls on His disciples to rely on Him — "Come to me," "Believe in me." He repeatedly assures them of his presence and guidance: "I shall be with you, even to the ends of the earth" (Matt. 28:20). One can easily see why thousands of our countrymen flock to gurus like Satya Saibaba. One of the secrets of his success is this assurance he gives them: "Do not fear, I am here." One constantly hears this or reads it on the walls of the Ashram temple, in his books, speeches, etc. So, too, other gurus and spiritual leaders constantly led their disciples to realize that they were/are never alone; therefore, they have nothing to fear. Ramana Maharishi, whose presence is palpably felt in his ashram even today, though he "left his body," said: "I am not going away, where could I go? I am here."[7] St. Paul could cry fearlessly, "If God be for us (with us), who is against us?" Did not Jesus Himself take courage from the fact that He was "not alone"? He who sent me is with me; he has not left me alone" (Jn. 8:29). But like us, his hearers, too, "did not understand" (Jn. 8:27). And they continued to be in fear in the darkness of *avidya*, for to be in the light fully or to have true *Vidya* is to believe and understand that "I am He" or "I am." And this takes us much further; more inward.

7. "It is I" (Jn. 6:20)

Jesus' words of reassurance, which also appear in the Synoptic version, probably represent the chief importance of this "sign." "It is I" — Lit: "I am" (ego). There are eight instances in John where Jesus identifies Himself absolutely with "I Am" (6:20; 8:24, 28, 58; 13:19; 1:85, 6, 8). Other "I Am" statements have a predicate — (6:35, 51; 8:12; 9:5; 10:7,9; 10:11, 14; 14:6; 15:1, 5.) John sees in this simple answer deep significance and understandably so. For here lies the heart, the center of all *jnan*, true wisdom, the secret of sanctity and total lasting happiness, for which alone man is made. "It is I." In Indian spirituality this word would be considered a *Mahavakya* to be repeated as a mantra and pondered on within the heart. Might one not see it as the counterpart or echo of the Upanishadic *Mahavakya* — *Aham Brahmasmi* — to be transformed by meditation and honest living later into *Aham Asmi* and still later, simply into *Aham* without any predicate?

This "It is I" begins thus with a series of "I am" tests without any predicate, though Jesus had already used the same verbal form to the Samaritan woman to show that he was the expected Messiah: "I who speak to you am He" (4:26). This saying "I am" (one can never tire of saying it) is of highest importance not only in John, but indeed in the whole Bible. For it amounts to using the name of Yahweh Himself (Exod. 3:14). John no doubt uses it deliberately to show the nature and mission of Jesus. It was a name blasphemous for any one to use. Babylon was condemned by Isaiah for appropriating this title to herself (47:8, 10). Yet John shows that it was not blasphemous for the Word Incarnate to use it. For him it was not simply what it was for the Synoptics. They saw in this miracle that accompanied the words "a stage in the disciples' growing awareness of the character of Jesus."[8] Truly you are the Son of God," they said (Matt. 14:33), though Mark adds that they yet "had not understood the real meaning of the feeding of the five thousand; their minds could not grasp it" (6:52).

And if they could not understand the real meaning of his "signs," who can blame them if "their minds could not grasp" the significance of this word of the Word? For as the Upanishads constantly teach, He is beyond the grasp of the intellect. "Not through much learning is the Atman reached, not through the intellect and sacred teaching" (Katha. Up. 2.23), and again, "He is the Atman," that cannot be seen or touched, that is above all distinction, beyond thought in ineffable. In union with Him is the supreme proof of His reality (Manduk. Up. 7). And his name is *Tadvanam*, which translated means "the End of all love-longing" (Kena. 4.6).

Have not Christian mystics known and taught as much? "Of God Himself can no man think. Therefore I will leave on one side everything I can think, and choose for my love that thing which I cannot think! Why? Because he may well be loved, but not thought. "By love he may be caught and held; by thinking never."[9] And yet we are constantly busy conceptualizing, thinking, reasoning. The Indian *rishi* (seer) and *jnani* (the wise) no less than Christian mystics know that it is only by sitting still and entering within, by self-inquiry, that one can ever hope to reach God. "One cannot know God by means of the mind. One can but turn the mind inwards and merge it in God."[10]

"Be still and know that I am God," as the Psalmist, too, truly puts it" (Ps. 46:10). To "know God" then becomes the same as knowing that "I am."

At first sight most Christians again tend to shrink away and find

themselves saying, "Beware! This smells of heresy! Are we not taught
by the church clearly that we are 'distinct' and not 'parts' of God; that
our identity as creatures must always be preserved and respected; that
we should keep clear of pantheism or of thinking ourselves as becoming
God?'' Yet the Bible has many passages — if one would dare to look
at them straight in the face — that tell us that God is in us, and therefore
that word *I am*, which He utters in us, becomes our own. To quote
only one saying, which Paul calls the test of our very faith: "Examine
yourselves to make sure you are in the faith; test yourselves." And
what does He give us as the criterion? Not believing all that one has
heard, or been taught, but rather, "Do you acknowledge that Jesus Christ
is really in you? If not, you have failed the test" (2 Cor. 13:5). Christians are called to experience this Oneness — this "I am," equally with
the Hindu, who calls it the Vedantic experience. The *antar-yatra, antaryami sadhana* — the ascesis of going within to hear and know and be
the "I am" of God is a call given to all men. Eckhart knew it and Tauler
and Ruysbroeck. And as the Lord said to Catherine of Siena, "The
creature is *not*"; only God is, and there is no one else beside Him,
before Him, or after Him, who could say of Him that "He is" or "He
alone is."[11] *Asti* He is! Ands nothing greater is there to be said or known.
As long as God remains for us "another," we can give Him names
(other than "I am"). Once one has understood Our Lord's "I Am,"
there is no one left even to say "Thou" until our "I" — all that makes
an individual in men's eyes — has been swallowed for good in the overwhelming experience of Him who alone IS, we do not really perceive
the meaning of his "It is I" — any more than His disciples were able
to. We have ultimately to lose our "I," our *ahamkar* or ego and become
His "I," i.e., become Him, till with Paul we can truly say, "I love,
no longer I, but Christ in me" (Gal. 2:20). And Tirumular, the Tamil
poet, had enough *vivek* (discrimination) to see that God's "I" is His
Love. Speaking of Shiva (the kindly or gracious One), he says:

> Shiva is one thing. Love is another.
> What ignorance to talk like that!
> What is Shiva? What is Love?

Who can ever know except him alone who, in the depth of his heart,

has wholly become Shiva, has wholly become Love, and so at last has
understood that Shiva is Love and Love is Shiva. And, we may add,
so at last has understood the "It is I."

Soham, Shivoham, Saccidanandsvaroopoham! ",'I am He, I am
Shiva, I am Saccidananda." By repeating these and surrendering to His
grace, one gradually comes to the *sahaja* awareness which persists
beneath and beyond all outward activites — the latter being like new
notes blending with the *adharsruti* or the fundamental note which remains sounding all the time. Even the remotest. . . caverns of his heart
turn out to be occupied already and the darkness in which he had hoped
to save his personal existence from annihilation in Being is already ablaze
with the glory of God. He still struggles desperately to utter an "I,"
a "Thou,"; but now no sound makes itself heard. . . It is immediately
submerged in the one "I am" that fills eternity. . . the immensity of
waters.[12] "The Lord's voice resounding on the waters, the Lord on
the immensity of waters" (Ps. 28:3).

8. And immediately the boat reached land (Jn. 6:21)

John says the disciples "wanted to take him into the boat" (they
willingly took him into the boat — Good News translation), though actually according to some scholars,[13] John does not make it clear whether
Jesus entered the boat. (According to the Synoptics, He did.) His emphasis is on the disposition of the disciples. Nor is it clear if by "im-
mediatley" or "suddenly," John means this to be another miraculous
event; probably he does so intend.

However that may be, John brings out the significance of this "sign"
of Jesus' walking on the waters only at the end of the discourse-on-the-
Eucharist which follows it. Peter's confession in answer to Jesus'
question to his disciples: "Will you also leave me?" (v. 67) is "Lord,
to whom shall we go? You have the words of eternal life." This is
probably understood by John as the equivalent of the Synoptics' episode
in Mark 8:27 ff ("What about you? Who do you say that I am?" "You
are the Messiah.")

Jesus had asked whether the disciples also "wish" [*thelete*] to depart
from Him (cf. v. 21, according to which they "wished" *ethlon* to receive

Him into the boat.) John now arrives at the final significance of this "sign" of Jesus walking on the waters. Our Lord's discourse on eternal life had scandalized many and they walked away from Him. Jesus' twelve disciples, however, chose not to leave Him and acknowledged that the word of God truly leads to eternal life.

"Wishing" to walk away from Jesus or "wishing" Him into our boat! Herein lies the difference and the mystery of life eternal. For our "boat" is but our heart. It is only by acknowledging Him in the cave of the heart that one finds Oneness and Life. It is only there that one finds "the waters of life" gushing forth and hears the "I" on the "immensity of waters." If we wish, we can turn within, tune in and hear the constant "I," the one; the "I am" that fills eternity; That *Tat* which Is *Sat*. *Om Tat Sat* (B. Gita 17.23). That "I" is, as Ramana Maharishi used to say, like the fundamental *sruti*, the *sa*. Other various notes of music may come and go, but the "I" continues, the note that underlies and blends with all other notes. Anyone who has caressed the *tanpura* (tambura) near the ear as he has sung Indian classical music, or anyone who has sat long enough or still enough by the Gangaji and heard her constant *Om* beneath and beyond all other sounds made by the waves or the winds, will understand this. But one has to choose — "wish" — to turn inwards. For if one wishes to "walk away"' from the cave of the heart and turn outwards[14] one might miss that "I am," miss Jesus walking on the waters.

One might — in the truest sense — "miss the boat" and fail to reach "the Further Shore Beyond Darkness" (Mund. Up. 2.2.6).

9. "The Further Shore"

The great lesson then and the true significance of this "sign" of Jesus walking on the waters is to teach us the secret of reaching the Further Shore where there is only one "I"; the only "I" that can speak the ultimate meaning of Life, the Self beyond the self. For there is the conditioned, limited ego or *ahamkar* which we all are familiar with and very fond of. But there is also the Unconditioned, Unlimited Self, the Spirit, the *Ātman*, who alone can give infinite bliss, for the Spirit is *Ānandam*. To attain to the awareness [*Chit*] of this Self or Being who is *Sat* and to attain to this fullness of bliss *Ānandam* is to be One; one with the Triune God, one with Sat-Chit-Anand. The Muslim mystic knew the same mystery, though he expressed it differently.

> I saw my lord with my heart's eye and said:
> "Who art Thou, Lord?" "Thyself," he replied...
> ...Is there an I *and* a Thou? That would make two Gods!
> One Selfhood is there, Thine, forever,
> At the heart of my nothingness.[15]

Thus "the heart of my nothingness" has to be reached and this is not easy.

This process of "journey inwards" to the Further Shore takes time and much pain. Now to leave our familiar shore, to say good bye to the little self, the "I" one has grown so fond of, is as painful as death. *Partir, c'est mourir un peu* is most true here! Only here it is total death to self. Here, diminishment is the law of life. The Baptist by the waters of Jordan knew it — "He (the Self) must increase; I (the little self) must decrease" (Jn. 3:30). In the measure in which the ego dies, the Self thrives. For this one has to have courage. But then for the man who realizes the Atman, knowing I am He, what craving or what urge could cause him to cling to the body? (Brihad U. 4.4.12).

When Peter wanted to walk on the waters, however, Jesus called him to do so. (John omits this incident in this miracle but cf. Matt. 14:28-33.) When "he felt the force of the wind, he took fright and began to sink." What caused him to cling to the body? Perhaps he thought of his goal as out there. Another, towards whom he had to walk, rather than of his own Self within, the *Antāryami* (The Indwelling controller) by whose power he could walk on the water. He was still in *avidya*!

Avidya consists of a sense of separateness, otherness, duality. *Duality engenders fear.* The Upanishads consistently teach that when a man sees the Atman, the Self in Him, God himself, "the Lord of what was and of what shall be, he fears no more." "Do not be afraid. It is I," Jesus said. That is reaching the Further Shore — having crossed the waters of egoism and having found the One Self, within or without. Indeed, there is no more a within or without. There is only One Self. "Egos are different and numerous as bubbles. The Self is One alone, like the ocean"[16] — like the multitudinous waters.

The voice of Yahweh over the waters! (Yahweh means "I Am".)

Yahweh over the multitudinous waters!
The voice of Yahweh is power!
The voice of Yahweh is splendor! (Ps. 29:32-4)

"It is I — Do not be afraid!"

Psalm 29:32-34

CHAPTER SEVEN

Water to Drink

If any man thirsts, let him come to me and drink:
He who believes in Me, out of his heart shall flow
streams of living water, as Scripture says.
He was speaking of the Spirit...John 7:37-39

Man thirsts, and if he is to continue living, this thirst must be quenched by water. Jyoti Sahi puts the first two of the above verses as the text to accompany his painting of the Samaritan woman drawing waters of life from the cave of Christ's heart. The two texts, John 4:14 and 7:37-38, are inextricably linked, as though the latter were exemplified and illustrated by the story of the Samaritan woman at the well of Jacob. For this reason we shall also link the two inevitably.

1. The context

Jesus' promise of living water was made in a loud voice. "He cried out," St. John tells us, "on the last day of the festival" (7:37). "The festival" was the feast of tabernacles which formed the background of these tremendous words. The liturgy of this feast included prayers for rain, rites which commemorated the Moasic water miracle (Ex. 17:1-7; cf. 1 Cor. 10:4) and other biblical passages foretelling life-giving water for Zion (Zac. 14:8; Ezek. 47:1, etc.).

Speaking of the ideological literary context in which Jesus speaks these words, Pierre Grelot explains how these libations at the water's gate on this feast of tents, arise from the Genesis myth of 2:10[1], where the water sprang from Eden to water the garden and divided itself into four several streams. The legend of the well recalls Ezek. 47:11-12, echoes Genesis, as though the original waters which made the earth fruitful were hidden because of man's sin, and reappear for the first time in the desert and then finally in the eschatological Jerusalem. "Along the river on either bank will grow every kind of fruit tree with leaves that never wither and fruit that never fails," and "wherever the water goes it brings health, and teems wherever the river flows" (Ezek. 47:12-9).

2. Life starts from water

The Hebrew poets were familiar with this water symbolism and the Psalms repeatedly remind us of what a vital role water played at the beginning of life. So, too, the early Vedic rishis tell us how our very life depends on it. Just a couple of quotations from both the biblical and Vedic texts will illustrate this.

> Splitting rocks in the wilderness, quenching their thirst with unlimited water, conjuring streams from the rock and bringing down water in torrents.
>
> Ps. 78:15-16

> Like cold water to a thirsty soul, so is good news from a far country.
>
> Ps. 25:25

In the Hindu Scriptures, too, water is referred to as the source and life of man:

> When came the mighty Waters, bringing with them the Universal
> Germ[2] whence sprang the Fire, thence leapt God's One Spirit into
> being.
>
> Rig Veda X.127.7

Incidentally, it is interesting to note how the Spirit, symbolized in
Christian tradition by fire and water, is often spoken of in similar terms
in Hindu mythology:

> He with clear flames shines bountiful on us without fuel in the
> waters (Rig ved. II.35.4); Apam Napat is thought of as the
> terrestrial Agni appearing on the sacrificial altar.

> He the son of waters, gathering strength within the waters, shines
> forth for the granting of wealth, to the advantage of the worshipper.
>
> Rig Ved. II.35.7

And so the waters are asked for their blessing again and again:

> May the celestial waters, our helpers, be sweet to our taste and
> shower on us blessing.
>
> Yajur ved. XXXIV.12

> These waters be to us for drink, Devine are they for aid and joy.
> May they impart to us health and strength.
>
> Rig Ved. X.9.4

Not only is life shown to start with waters — both in the biblical
and Vedic traditions,but water is thus a giver of health, joy, refreshment, especially to man stranded and athirst. Thus Yahweh's salvific
activity for Israel is compared in the Old Testament to the water being
produced in the desert.

> Waters shall break forth in the wilderness and streams in the desert;
> the burning sand shall become a pool and the thirsty grounds springs
> of water.
>
> Is. 35:6-7

And again:

> I will open rivers on the bare heights and fountains in the midst

of the valleys. I will make the wilderness a pool of water and the dry land springs of water.

Is. 41:18

In Jeremiah 2:13 Yahweh calls Himself the fountain of living water and Jesus astounds his hearers by taking Yahweh's place as it were in promising the gift of living water — both in John 4:14 and 7:37. "Let (who thirsts) come to Me and drink." One can imagine the electric shock the Jews must have received on hearing this! It would be somewhat like the stunning effect that would be provoked in orthodox Hindu hearts if a man by the Ganga kinara were to announce that they need no longer drink of or bathe in the Ganges, but instead come to him and drink!

3. "On the last day of the festival"

It is not clear whether this day was the seventh day — when like the previous six days of the feast, water was brought in golden flagon from the pool of Siloe to be used for libations, or whether it refers to the eighth day when, as Marsh points out, the nonperformance of the rite would focus attention even more pointedly on Our Lord's words. He would then take the place of the water required by the old Jewish rituals, as the source of real, life-sustaining power which he could give to those who believe in Him. In any case, the occasion was solemn, festal, momentous.[3]

4. If anyone thirst

It is not any particular type of person, with special background or qualities whose thirst will be slaked. Anyone at all can approach the Master. He is available to any and all. Only they must be thirsty. And who in this world is not athirst for happiness? Yet how few understand that real and lasting happiness can only be found in the eternal, not in the transitory things that give but incomplete happiness and still leave us thirsting for something! This thirst must then be for God, who alone can slake our thirst, for in Him alone is total and lasting bliss to be found. He is the Source and Completion of Joy. He is Bliss, *Ananda*, for which we are made. "Thou hast made us for thyself, O Lord," finally cried Augustine, who had tried running after all sorts of pleasures to slake his great heart's thirst and then admitted, "Our hearts are restless until they find their rest in Thee."

Mumukshutva is the last but most important of the four prerequisites demanded by Shankaracharya for the one desiring God — Realization.

> "As a heart longs for flowing streams, so longs my soul for Thee,
> O God (Ps. 42:1).

How can the waters of joy and love be given to one who is not thirsty? The same Spirit who is joy is love. One of the messages of the Upanishads is that the Spirit can only be known to him who thirsts for union with him, not through mere learning. "Not through much learning is the Atman reached, not through the intellect and sacred teaching. It is reached by the chosen of Him" (Katha Up. 2.23). No amount of learning can make us feel love or see beauty that will satisfy forever. The Eternal cannot be grasped by the transient sense or the mind. "Words and mind go to him but reach him not and return. Only the Eternal can lead us to the Eternal; only when the transient has become Eternal can a man say, "I am He,"[4] and thus have his thirst completely slaked. This thirst must then be truly great, ardent — "like the desire of one set on fire to throw himself into a nearby pool." That is his one and only desire at that moment. Nothing else, however glittering or alluring, will distract or draw a man in such straits away from that *Ekāgrāta* or One-pointedness of his thirst. For this reason Jesus, too, asks first for man to be thirsty; though he may not always realize that he is thirsting for God. Jesus proceeds to show that He is the Source that will surely and unfailingly satisfy man's inherent thirst of the spirit and so he invites:

5. "Let him come to me and drink; He who believes in Me"

Jesus shows the people present at this festival what he had said to the Samaritan woman at the well, viz. that He is the real quenching of their thirst. "Coming" to him means having faith in Him. One has only to read cursorily through any of the four Gospels to see the importance and vital necessity of faith. Without faith nothing is achieved; no miracle is worked, no salvation attained. To "come" to Jesus means to come with the conviction that He can and will provide what is wanting. And if their thirst is of the spirit, all the more surely; for physical thirst, however dreadful and critical, is but a metaphor or symbol of spiritual thirst.

6. "Out of his heart shall flow streams of living water"

There is a puzzle about these words of Jesus, i.e., Does the "heart" refer to the Lord's heart or to that of the one who drinks? Either could be right, though I prefer the latter interpretation. It is briefly put, by Marsh, as follows:

Is this a well-known form of Jewish poetry, with a balanced symmetry of expression, or is it somewhat more awkward in form, repeating the teaching of John 4:14 about a spring of water welling up in the believer? The text of the RSV translation has assumed the latter solution, which is probably the right one. Origen and some of the Eastern Fathers interpreted it this way. But the alternative would read: "If anyone thirst, let him come to me, and let him who believes in me drink." "This is certainly a neater piece of syntax and it has a further advantage of allowing the following words to be taken, if that seems necessary, with what follows rather than with what has preceded." Then the words "Out of his heart shall flow rivers of living water" need not apply to the believer, and that would be a relief to the Old Testament student who would find it impossible to cite a quotation making such a statement. But it must be pointed out that the difficulty of finding a suitable scripture quotation, even if the words be applied to Christ, is still apparently insoluble."[5]

Whichever of the two interpretations of biblical scholars may be right, for the reader who wished to do *nididhyāsanam* (contemplating the Word in the silence of the stilled heart) and not stop merely at *Mananam* (reflecting over the meaning of the text at the mind-level), as many of us Christians are wont to do, either interpretation or both can yield much sweetness. St. Ignatius, speaking of contemplating the Word, had taught: *"Non abundantia scientiae sed sentire et gustare res interne."* This approach (of wanting to "feel and taste the inner thing" rather than an abundance of knowledge about the text) would be far nearer, too, to the Indian way of letting the *jnan* be transformed into *vijnan*, as the Word is allowed to pass fro the active mind, after it had been fully used, to the silent and loving heart. Here the text would yield joy and light, whether the living water is seen as issuing from the Heart of Christ (as later in John 19:34; cf. Rev. 22:1) or as springing from the believer's heart. The one who has already drawn lovingly and longingly from His Heart *("puiser dans Son Coeur"* as the French Saint Madeleine Sophie loved to say) is able then to pass on the water to others — like the Samaritan Woman. "Come and see the man," she went and told others of her village. "Could he be the Messiah?" (Jn. 4:29) Thus Jyoti Sahi, the artist-theologian in the painting already referred to, portrays the woman who has been drawing from the cave of Christ's heart with ardent longing — depicted by her entire figure drawn, as it were, upwards and into Christ, till she is standing on her toes, being herself transformed into a stream of water so that it becomes evident that the heart of the drinker is no more separate from the heart of Him who is the Source. The water is the same. The canal that passes on the water is but an instrument, not the Source.

7. Out of His "Heart"

Some writers have even suggested that once the connection with the believer is given up, the quotation can be taken as referring to Jerusalem. In eschatological Old Testament literature, the theme of Jerusalem as a source of living waters is common. "When that day comes, running waters will issue from Jerusalem" (Zech. 14:8; cf. Ezek. 47:1-12). This figure could easily have been extended to the dweller in the eschatological Jerusalem.[6] Thus Isaiah says, "You shall be as a watered garden, like a spring of water whose waters never run dry" (58:11).

"Heart" in the Revised Standard Version of the Bible is "belly" in the AV and the RV. But "belly" in the Old Testament can be a synonym for "navel" and Jerusalem is sometimes called the "navel" of the world. The writers who spoke of the centrality of Jerusalem in the final order which God would inaugurate, sometimes pictured Jerusalem as the center from which flowed life-giving streams of water bringing fertility to the whole outside world.[7] A stream came out from under the temple threshold and teemed wherever the river flowed. This image of miraculous water from the Temple conferring a miraculous fertility is later resumed in Rev. 22:2. On either side of the river were the trees of life, the leaves of which are the cure for pagans. The Temple could be a symbol, too, of His Heart, as also "the city of God" in Psalm 96:4. "There is a river whose streams refresh the city of God, and it sanctifies the dwelling of the Most High." This "dwelling" could again be God's Heart as well as man's heart — which is rightly called the Temple of God — in which dwells the *Antaryami* — the Indwelling Spirit.

For the man "who believes in Me" — It is the heart from which a joyous outpouring of God will issue; for a true believer life is full of joy and excitement. If it is not, it shows that there is something wrong either with his faith or his idea of God. It is perhaps due to this lack that not many today are men of good and stout hearts. The heart has grown old and arthritic. The joy, the bounce, the intellectual ability and adventurousness have gone. The Greek theologians found God enormous fun. "Our present social revolution is throwing up a class highly empowered by new money and considerable intelligence, in whom this vastly and suddenly increased scope makes painfully evident by contrast, the lack of real center, a heart quickened to life. They are people who experience an immense amount of life and do not find life exciting. The heart, unable to grow to this situation, is instead stunned by it into a stunted and fearful state. In terms of such people, it is not difficult to define the requirements for a valid God-concept. God is the excitement which life for these people does not have."[8] Their conversion will require that they find their center, their heart, first, then they will find God in the center of their heart and not divorced from their life. "For a staid and fearful orthodoxy is at pains to keep God distinct from the human flourishing that is, nevertheless, according to real Christian orthodoxy, his most authentic manifestation in the flesh."[9]

The heart is the center and the source in man. The Tamil sage and saint Ramana Maharishi, whose brief "death experience" led to Self-Realization, often referred to the importance and centrality of the heart.

His method of realization, inquiring "Who am I?" led to the true nature
of the Self of Atman (Spirit). He used to say that this constant inquiry
would lead the mind "back to its source" and that as thought subsided
with repeated practice, the mind would learn to stay in its source, i.e.,
in its heart. There and thus man would find his true Self.

8. He was speaking of the Spirit

The evangelist explicitly adds that this saying ("the water that I
shall give him") was really about the Spirit, who had not been given
as Jesus was not yet glorified (7:39). Obviously it does not, cannot,
mean (as some say the literal Greek could indicate) "the Spirit was not
yet," for the Spirit existed from before the Incarnation — in fact, from
before time was. Mark quotes Jesus as saying that David was inspired
by the Holy Spirit (Mk. 12:36) and Luke preserves for us the words
of Jesus: "How much more will the Heavenly Father give the Holy
Spirit to those who ask Him?" (11:23) "Not yet been given" here means,
then, that the Spirit has not yet come in the fullness of His power.

John's insistence upon the Crucifixion — Exaltation (glorification)
of Jesus before the Spirit could be outpowered has been compared, at
least in essential respects, to the synoptist's insistence that a man can
only be a true disciple of Christ if he shares his cross. Marsh says, "No
cross, no crown" is a proposition as true of the Lord's disciple as of
the disciple's Lord. Only in the sharing of the destiny of the Lord does
the disciple acquire the power to become himself, in and with his Lord,
a source of life-giving power. The Christian's overflowing spirit of
humility, victory, and joy cannot be obtained directly, but only in sharing, with Christ, in the agonies of redemption.[10] John is writing from
an end perspective, from a Church perspective, and that the Spirit cannot be sent till Christ be glorified, is a theological, not a chronological,
fact.

Thus in John "living water" does not mean so much "revelation"
(as it did in the Wisdom books) nor "Torah" (as it did in the Rabbinic
tradition), but rather "the Holy Spirit". When he spoke to the Samaritan
Woman of the living water that would become a "spring welling up
to eternal life" (4:14), this particular activity of "welling up" *(hallesthai)*

is similar to the activity of the Spirit described in the Old Testament as an eruption of the Holy Spirit upon men. "He shall come as a pent-up stream, impelled by the breath of Yahweh" (Is. 59:19). Lucius Nereparampil says that "living water" can only symbolize grace which is the outcome of the activity of the Spirit which interiorizes the words in man. "The dynamism or the welling up of the water is nothing but the activity of the Spirit received in man's interior,"[11] the Spirit who is the interiority of God, and dwells in the innermost heart of man.

9. Spirit and heart; Spirit and self

It may throw more light on this biblical text to see the same thing in Vedantic terms. One would then say that the Spirit (symbolized by the "living waters" that flow out of the heart, whether of Christ or of the believer) is the Atman who abides in the heart, "in the space of the heart." The Atman or Spirit is very closely linked with the heart. The Spirit of Christ is the Spirit of his heart. "The Atman dwells within the heart. Its etymology is explained in this way: "It dwells within the heart; therefore it is called heart." He who knows this proceeds daily to the world of heaven (Chandog Up. VIII 3.3). "This great unborn Atman who is the spiritual element among the life-powers dwells in that space within th heart the Ordainer of all, the Lord of all, the Ruler of all (Brihad Up. IV 22). The *Sandilya Wisdom* tells us the same truth: "He is my Atman, within the heart, smaller than a grain of rice, smaller than a grain of barley, a grain of mustard or a grain of millet. He is my Atman within the heart, greater than the earth, greater than the sky, greater than heaven itself and all these worlds. He contains all works, all desires, all perfumes, all tastes. . . He is my Atman within my heart; he is Brahma. On departing from here, I shall merge with him" (Chandog Up. XIV 3.4).

The Spirit of Atman is the "One-ing" Principle — not only within God (as Christian revelation of the Trinity makes clear) but also uniting man to God and making the two one, till there is no more duality (cf. Jn. 17:26) — till man sees only God and nothing as separate from Him. The *Madhu Vidya* of the Brihadaranyaka Upanishad and the doctrine of the interdependence of all things — shows how the Purusha in the

cosmos and in man are the same, the Atman, the immortal Brahma.
This *advaita* (nonduality) of the Spirit is also found — in terms of water
— in the Katha Up:

> As water descending on mountain crags, wastes its energies among
> the gullies, so he who views things as separate, wastes his energies
> in their pursuit.

> But as pure water poured into pure, becomes the self-same —
> wholly pure, so, too, becomes the self of the silent sage, of the
> one, O Gautama, who has understanding.

IV 14-15

10. The Self and the self

Even at the risk of being thought of as "meandering away from
Johannine theology of the Spirit," I should like to venture a little thinking
aloud. For how else will Indian theologizing be encouraged to evolve,
unless some are ready to make fools of themselves — or be made fools
of — for Christ's sake? Now it seems to me — though I stand under
correction — that it is the Spirit who is the Self who burns up the little
self in man. For as long as a man has a strong sense of his own ego
— the *ahamkar* (literally the I-maker), God is necessarily Another for
him. To him the I-Thou relationship is all; *advaita* can only mean a
mere intellectual concept and not an actual experience, and it has been
pointed out that it might have a disastrous effect on the disciple and
increase his self-concept and egoism, if the guru were to introduce him
to *advaita* before he was prepared for it. The true guru will not begin
by revealing the heights of *advaita* experience at the very start, just
as Jesus the Satguru did not teach his disciples straightaway about the
Spirit or his unifying role in their lives. Only towards the end of His
ministry did He speak of the Spirit and even then, cautiously. "I still
have many things to say to you, but they would be too much for you
now" (Jn. 16:12)

For this reason the guru will prepare his disciples by the entire gamut
of yogic disciplines — silencing the mind, learning to withdraw it by
pratyahara (withdrawal from things of sense); by fixing one-pointed

attention on a single object through *dharana* (concentration), learning this *Ekagrata* or One-pointedness through constant *namjap* (repetition of God's name), etc. Only then will the disciple be ready to absorb and realize the teaching of the One-ing Spirit, and that "No one is different from or other than myself,' as the Narada Parivraajaka Up. says (4.38). Then, knowing experimentally that no one at all is other to himself, his heart overflows — with living water — "with the unique experience of his own being" (Pa.Na.Fa.Up. 4.38).

11. "Who sees all beings in his own self" (Isa. Up. 6)

When a man is thus so filled and possessed by the Spirit, he sees everywhere God and nothing but God. Not only the *jnani* but also the *bhakta* is meant to reach this state of oneness. Many a *bhajan* (hymn) sings of this seeing, as in the famous one by Mirabai:

> *Andar Rama, bahar Rama*
> *Jahan dekho vahan Rama hi Rama.*
> (Whether I turn, within or without
> Wherever I look, I see only Ram)

Innumerable poems and lovesongs to the Lord can be found in the various Indian languges which indicate the same truth — viz. that God, who is Spirit, dwells within and without.

"He is far and He is near. He is within all, He is outside all" (Isa. Up. 5). This supreme Upanishadic truth contemplated by *Jnanis* and sung by *bhaktas* and experienced by both, is promised by Jesus as the work of his Unifying Spirit of Love, who makes all truth complete and clear (Jn. 16:13), who is the Love that unites the Father and Son and makes man's heart his abode (Jn. 17:26), in order to be his very Self.

12. The theology of Ananda in-Oneness

"The man who realizes the Atman, knowing 'I am He' — what craving or what urge could cause him to cling to the body?" (Brihad.

Up. IV 4:12). "Who sees all beings in his own Self and his own Self in all beings, loses all fear. When a sage sees this great Unity and his Self has become all beings, what delusion and what sorrow can even be near him?" (Isa. Up. 6-7). Only joy and bliss eternal. This is also what Jesus has been leading his disciples to. Those "who believe in Him," who drink from His side whence overflowed the living waters of the Spirit, were to experience only peace and joy.

"I have told you this, so that my own joy may be in you and your joy be complete" (Jn. 15:11). And again, "while still in the world I say these things to share my joy with them to the full" (Jn. 17:13). His own joy is the Spirit of bliss — Ananda. For God is Joy, the Source and Goal of all lasting joy — for which man so acutely thirsts. This is what after much *tapas* (asceticism) and "spiritual Prayer" Bhrigu Varuni saw and understood: that "Brahman is joy; from joy all beings have come; by joy they all live; and unto joy they all return" (Taitt. Up. III 1.6). Moltman, speaking somewhere of the theology of joy, says that when we cease using God as "Helper-in-need," "stop-gap," "problem-solver," we are finally free for the joy of God and of enjoyment of each other in God. This uniquely satisfying bliss can only be given and taught us by the Spirit whom Jesus promised and poured out on man — the joy that can come only in finding Oneness who is God, finding His unique Self everywhere. This unification by the Spirit is what Jesus prayed for in his final sacerdotal prayer:

"May they all be one" — not just that all Christians and all men may be united among themselves and stop squabbling; but that man may have the courage to "drink" from Him so deeply that he may become joyously one with God and with all forever. It was "John's invitation to the secret descent into the depths of one's own heart, towards that Glory which was even before creation in the pre-existing Word."[12]

> "May they all be one, Father, may they be one in us, as You are in Me and I am in You, So that the world may believe it was You who sent Me. I have given them the glory you gave to me, that they may be one as we are One. With Me in them and You in Me, May they be so completely One that the world will realize that it was You who went me and that I have loved them as much as You loved me" (Jn. 17:21-23).

But this the world would not accept — any more than the Jews accepted Jesus' cry "If any man thirsts let him come to me and drink." It shocked them and "scandalized" them as that other *advaitic* word of his: "The Father and I are One" (Jn. 10:30) or "Before Abraham ever was, I am" (Jn. 8:58).

And this word led to a division among men. In fact the whole of the seventh chapter of St. John — before and after this verse — deals with the discussions about Who Jesus was. "Some said, 'He is a good man;' others, 'No, he is leading the people astray.' People stood whispering about him in groups." (7:12). They discussed the origin of the Messiah, "Can it be true that the authorities have made up their minds that he is the Christ? Yet we all know where he comes from..." (7:26-27). "They would have arrested Him, but no one touched Him for His hour had not yet come" (7:30). In spite of knowing of this mounting tension, Jesus had boldly "cried out" this invitation at the Temple telling how the Spirit would be poured out. After this boldly wondrous and mighty declaration, there were further discussions on the origin of the Messiah. "Surely he must be the prophet and some said "He is the Christ." Others said, "Would the Christ be from Galilee?" (7:40-41). "The temple police who had heard this invitation to drink from Him and had been sent to arrest Him, returned to the Chief Priests and Pharisees; and when questioned, "Why haven't you brought him?" answered, "There has never been anybody who has spoken like Him" (7:44-46). When these Pharisees damned the rabble who believed in Him, only one little brave voice was heard — that of the man who had come by night to Jesus and had had a private tuition on "water and the Spirit." He said, "Surely the law does not allow us to condemn a man without hearing him?" But they mocked him, "Are you a Galilean too? Go into the matter and see for yourself, prophets do not come out of Galilee" (Jn. 7:50-52).

The enraged Pharisees caricature this modest defense of Jesus in terms of regional prejudice. Are we not all familiar with this phenomenon in India? A South Indian saint acknowledged in Uttarkhand will often be looked at askance. "No Galilean prophet" could hardly mean that literally there had been no prophet from Galilee. John (2 Kings 14:25) and possibly also Hosea hailed from Galilee. John means that they were sufficiently carried away by anger to deny even obvious facts. They probably meant that the eschatological prophet of verse 40 was not to be a Galilean. Their reply suggests that any followers Jesus had obtained had come exclusively from the *amha ares*, the people of the land, who were not students of the law.[13] Nicodemus actually stands as a contradiction to their claims that no Pharisee had been affectd by Jesus' teaching.

Conclusion

"Go into the matter and see for yourself."

This is what one has to do — on hearing Jesus' invitation to come to him and drink. Only so will our thirst be quenched by these living waters he offers us. Only so will we have the courage to "see" the Self in the *Advaita* of the Spirit whom he pours out. But to "go into the matter" will require courage; it will involve dying to the small self. It may mean taking the risk of being condemned by all the Pharisees of our times, by all who are important and significant. Only so will our thirst be fully quenched. No other waters will satisfy — only the waters of life, that is, the Spirit poured out of the broken heart of Christ.

CHAPTER EIGHT

The Guru's Pad-Puja

John 13:1-20

In some Hindu ashrams every Thrusday, which is called *guruvar* (the day of the guru) there is a ceremony of *Guru-pad-puja*, when the disciples wash the feet of the guru, anoint them, and offer flowers and gifts as his feet. If the guru has already "left his body" or passed out of this world,[1] they perform this ceremony at his *paduka*; two feet or sandals made in stone or metal which symbolize the presence of the guru. In our own Christian ashram we observe a similar rite on Thursdays in memory of Christ's *pad-puja* and wash each other's feet, for Jesus the Satguru, instead of having his feet washed, as would be expected, Himself washed the feet of his disciples and told them to do as He had done — a symbolic gesture showing their willingness to serve and love, which means their willingness to die.

Water is used here by Our Lord to teach us some very significant lessons for our spiritual life. It is used as a symbol of glorification — death-resurrection — of a knowledge that is love. And love means emptying of one's self, which can be done veery practically and effectively through service of karma-yoga, a loving that knows no bounds or boundaries and which ultimately washes us pure enough to be able to see God in all people and places — even God kneeling at our feet.

1. Water and the theology of glorification

Water, God's favorite creature, is used first to teach us the "theology of glorification." Though John dates the Last Supper differently from the Synoptics, both affirm the fulfillment of the Jewish Passover in the events of Christ's death and resurrection. "It was before the feast of Passover and Jesus knew that the hours had come for him to pass from this world to the Father" (v. 1). For John this was the real passover; all the others wre but symbolic, for Jesus was the true Lamb of God offered for the world's sins on the Cross.

According to a Jewish tradition, the word *passover* [*pesah*, cf. Exod. 12:11] meant a passing or crossing over, referring to the crossing of the Red Sea (Exod. 14). Christ (and we with Him) will pass from this world, which is enslaved by sin, to the Father's company, the true Land of Promise (cf. Jn. 1:21).[2] It is interesting that "passing over" or crossing over to the "Further Shore" are expressions also found in Indian spirituality, indicating leaving this world of *samsara* and going to one's final liberation [*moksha*]. Thus is indicated the same idea of leaving behind the land and state of slavery and darkness and passing to to true freedom and light. By the expression "reaching the further shore" one also sees the idea of crossing waters — as in the Old Testament Yahweh had made his passage through the waters and He made the Israelites cross the Red Sea. "Blessings on your journey to the further shore beyond darkness" (Mund. Up. 2.2.6). One has to go through the darkness of death before reaching the Life of light as Christ did. This John calls his "glorification."

2. Jesus "knew" that He came from God and was going to God

Jesus knew that His hour of crossing had come (v. 1). He knew — in a way that transcended normal understanding — "that the Father had put everything into his hands and that he had come from God and was returning to God" (v. 3).

Indeed, we all have to know this; we are all on our way — returning

to the Source from whence we came, and only so, find our true home
and happiness.

The raindrops showered down by the clouds
Rose from the sea and will not rest
Until they reach, despite all hindrance,
Once again their ocean-home.

Ramana Maharishi — Ashtakam

Schillebeecks explains beautifully what this knowing Himself to
be *coming from God* — ''going forth from the Father'' — really meant
for Jesus. So truly did he become *Sarx* that he could say with us: ''Out
of the depths I have cried to Thee, O Lord'' — not in a local but in
a qualitative sense: ''Out of the depths of the miserable state of fallen
mankind, I call upon you, my God.'' This cry is ''the outburst of a
man who, even though knowing himself personally bound to the Father
in love from the depths of his human heart, was nevertheless living in
utter truth, through to the very end, the experience of the estrangement
from God belonging to our sinfulness, identifying himself with
everything there ever was, is or will be of sin-spawned alienation from
God in this world. He had to pass through the helplessness of this alienation from God to receive the glory the Father would give him. In
dispossessing himself of himself, Jesus hallowed himself to the Father
in whom he finds his exaltation and glory. And behind all this there
lies a mystery of unfathomable depth.''[3]

Jesus was not surprised nor dismayed at the course of events that
were to follow for his ''crossing over.'' What the experience of
omniscience might be, mere human beings cannot know. But it seems
plain that when omniopotence appears in the world, its all-conquering
power looks very much like impotence as it hangs upon a cross: it may
well be that omniscience as it embodied in the life of the Word-Made-
Flesh is as real and, to a mere mortal, as unrecognizable as omnipotence![4]

3. Knowing and loving — *prem-jnan*

Knowing meant showing his love ''unto the end.'' Knowledge that
does not fructify in love is but sterile. This is true even within God,

in his Triune life in God's knowledge of Himself (for knowing anything less than Himself would be unworthy of Him, "His thought," "His word," His consciousness" — all these are but various ways of saying the same thing). His knowledge spilled over as it were, in the bliss of Love that is the Holy Spirit, the *Anandam* of *Saccidananda*. This Knowledge — Love within God — is expressed in human, visible, tangible, to-us-understandable terms in the life of Jesus.

For Jesus "knew" and Jesus "loved" as no other. He was *Jnan-Bhakti* or *Prem-jnan* personified. The Word which is the Self-knowledge of God — breathed forth Love within the Trinity: *Verbum spirans amorem*, "The Word breathing forth love." This was the essence — the very nature of the Word — the *Shabda-Brahman* breathed forth his *pran*, the vital energy of love. "This is my commandment, a new commandment I give to you, that you love one another as I have loved you" (Jn. 13:34). The impression one gets is that the explicit expression of His love — love for His disciples — was a secret kept by Jesus for these last moments. (cf. Jn. 13:34; 15:9; 13; 17:23; Jn. 3:16; Gal. 2:20; Rom. 8:35; Eph. 3:19; 5:2, 25.) The great Old Testament teaching of the first two commandments on love were to be exemplified and taught in Jesus' life. To love God and to love one's neighbor as oneself were kindred commandments. Here suffice it to say that Jesus was about to show first symbolically, and then very concretely, unto shedding of His blood — what love could and should mean. John clearly states for the first time that Christ's life and death are an expression of His love for His disciples. "He had always loved those who were his in the world, but now he showed how perfect his love was" (v. 1); literally he loved them to the end, i.e., utterly, to the utmost. John states that what is to come is Jesus' final display of his love, or perhaps more likely, that it was a supreme exemplification of that love.[5] "To the end" also meant to that moment when the *eschaton*, the end, arrived.

4. "Jesus emptied Himself"

"They were at supper" (v. 2). Though John does not recount the institution of the Eucharist, one cannot but be aware of the signficance that this meal has in relation to Jesus' life. Hence John emphasizes this action as part of that significance. "Knowing that the Father had put everything into his hands," i.e., knowing his relationship to the Father, Jesus intends this act of feet-washing to be a concrete symbol of humiliation of his incarnational act. "He got up from the table, removed his outer garment, and taking a towel, wrapped it round his waist; he then poured water into a basin, and began to wash the disciples' feet and to wipe them with the towel he was wearing" (13:4-5). The dress and duty were clearly those of a slave. In 1 Samuel we read, for instance, how when David's servants came to Abigail at Carmel with an offer of marriage, "She rose and bowed down her face to the ground" — rather like we do the *panchang pranam* in India to those we want to honor and respect greatly. "Consider your servant a slave," she said "to wash the feet of my Lord's servants" (1 Sam. 25:40-42). The incident of the washing of the disciples' feet significantly follows immediately after the profound statements of Jesus about his origin and destiny. He has come from God and is going to God, and both journeys involve a voluntary humility. And both receive symbolic representation in the act of humble service now rendered. One can imagine the majesty, beauty, composure and solemnity with which Jesus rose to perform this work, usually done by a woman or a slave, the dignity and purposefulness with which He laid aside His garments and took up, girded Himself with a towel. It is pointed out how "laying aside" and "taking up" [the same Greek word *lithenai*] — is used for Jesus' death and resurrection (cf. Jn. 10:11, 15, 17 f.). Only He reverses here the role of the guru and the disciples.

St. Paul was later to tell the Christians at Philippi: "In your minds you must be the same as Christ Jesus. His state was divine, yet he did not cling to his equality with God, but emptied himself to assume the condition of a slave, and become as men are; and being as all men are, he was humbler yet, even to accepting death, death on a cross" (Phil. 2:5-8).

Jesus did not deem His equality with God as something to grasp and hold onto. Christ could not have surrendered His equality with God by nature. But He gave up what He could have chosen to keep — viz. being treated and honored as equal to God. Adam (and all his children after him) had wanted to be seen to be like God (Gen. 3:5, 22). But Jesus "emptied Himself," by giving up not His divine nature, which He could not, but the glory to which His divine nature entitled Him and which had been His before the Incarnation (Jn. 17:5). Normally speaking this glory would have been observable in His human body, as it was very occasionally, e.g., at His Transfiguration (Matt. 17:1-8). But He voluntarily deprived Himself of this, so that it could be returned to Him by His Father (cf. Jn. 8:50, 54) — after His sacrifice on the cross (cf. Phil. 2:9-11).[6]

5. "Not to be served but to serve"

This "emptying" of Himself was not true only of the Incarnation. Having made that fundamental option, Jesus, all through His life, continued to choose to be lowly rather than to be "high." In fact, this was one of the major points of his revolutionary teaching, turning values upside down. Men like to seek to be honored, esteemed, thought well of. When a dispute arose among his disciples — who were very normal human beings — as to who was to be reckoned the greatest among them, Jesus said, "Among pagans it is the kings who lord it over them, and those who have authority over them are given the title 'Benefactor.' This must not happen with you. No, the greatest among you must behave as if he were the youngest, the leader as if he were the one who serves. For who is the greater: the one at table or the one who serves? The one at table, surely? Yet here am I among you as one who serves!" (Lk. 22:24-27)

So, too, in Mark 10:42 we read of James and John on the way to Jerusalem, for the very last time in the life of Jesus, telling Him that their ambition was to sit on His right and left in heaven! Jesus answered them that they did not know what they were asking for and pointed out how very different their outlook was from his own. "For the Son of man came not to be served but to serve, and to give his life as a ransom for many." What a far cry form the devil's *non serviam*!

Jesus brought home the same lesson of humility in the parable of choosing places at table, for "he had noticed how they picked their places of honor. He said, "When someone invites you to a wedding feast, do not take your seat in the place of honor. . . No, when you are a guest, make your way to the lowest place and sit there, so that when your host comes he may say, "My friend, move up higher. . . For everyone who exalts himself will be humbled, and the man who humbles himself will be exalted" (Luke 14:7-11).

We are so familiar with these sayings of Jesus, as with the text of Philemon quoted above, that often we take them for granted. We are not shaken by the sheer wonder of it. Sometimes a biblical text like this comes alive when one considers it in the context not only of a non-biblical scripture-text (as we have often done in previous chapters) but even more if we see it in a non-Christian "living out" of it. Thus for me, for instance, this text, and the action of Jesus washing the feet of his disciples (which action could have occurred quite naturally in conjunction with this Lukan episode) came really alive when I saw a Hindu guru, esteemed as a man of God by thousands of disciples all over the world, not only himself constantly touching the feet of those who would approach him, wishing rather to prostrate themselves at his feet, but also serving them. This is very unusual; for most gurus, pandits, elders, teachers, parents allow their "inferiors" to touch their feet as a mark of respect, but would not dream of themselves touching their feet in return. Once I saw the same guru in a Christian ashram where he was invited, rising from his meal and asking to be allowed to serve us, saying: "The Lord Jesus washed the feet of his disciples. Let me at least be given the privilege of serving you." On another occasion the impact of the scene of Jesus' washing others' feet came home to me when I was watching the feet-washing, not of twelve clean, well-washed feet of boys or men sitting in the sanctuary of a church during a Maundy Thursday ceremony, nor of a monastic superior washing the feet of his/her community, but rather watching the Hindu guru washing the dirty, dusty feet of many Harijans on Gandhi Jayanti day.[7] For who more than Gandhiji had shown to our countrymen the true meaning and importance of *seva* (service) at cost to self?

6. Water of hospitality and of purification

The washing of feet was frequent and seems to have constituted one of the first gestures of hospitality in the Old Testament (cf. Gen. 18:4; Jud. 19:21, etc.) as indeed it does even today in many places in the East. One who came home from a journey first washed his feet

(2 Sam. 11:8). Sometimes a servant was appointed for this office (cf.
1 Sam. 25:41). In general, as for washing one's hands, in the East,
water is poured over the feet. One does not put the feet or hands into
a receptacle (2 Kings 3:11). Philippe Raymond in his study *"L'Eau,
sa vie et sa signification dans l'"ancien Testament"* points out how water
was used as spiritual purification for washings on other occasions such
as after a funeral (2 Sam. 12:20) and after one had cried (Gen. 43:31).
New-born children, too, were likewise washed (Ezek. 16:4).[8] "Jesus,
like a good Jew, kept the Jewish customs, though always with freedom
of heart, putting the spirit before the law. He even felt it when, as in
the house of Simon the Pharisee, this custom was not kept, and praised
the woman who with her tears had washed his feet where Simon had
failed to do so (cf. Lk. 7:36 f.). Water, his *creature cherie*, is involved
in several of these customs.

The water of the feet-washing, like the water of the wedding at
Cana in Galilee, has been made the symbol of the purification wrought
by the sacrificial death of Jesus, and by that alone. In this way the
washing of the feet enables the beloved community of Israel to understand both the baptism offered to the old community by John the Baptist
and the water turned into wine at the wedding which took place in the
old Israel; for now the real bridegroom of Israel has come to claim his
bride, making plain in the symbol of purificatory water with which Jesus
ministers to them,[9] that it is in and through his death that the new people
of God would be purified and kept clean. He was to explain this to Peter
who was, as always, slow to understand.

7. Do you wash my feet? (Jn. 13:6)

Peter protests as he sees Jesus approaching him to wash his feet.
It was too much for him. The incongruity of the situation — the Master
at the feet of the disciples — makes him cry out, "You will never wash
my feet" (v. 8). It is the feet — the lowest part of one's body — that
one touches in India as a sign of reverence. It is the feet that the Lord
touches and even washes. It is the feet that were washed, according
to the oriental custom, not only because, after walking the dusty roads,
they were the part of the body that most needed cleansing and refresh

ment, but also because one is not worthy — as the Baptist declared about Christ — to touch anything more than the feet of a holy person, of an elder or a better: "I am not fit to undo his sandal-strap" (Jn. 1:27). Peter is still looking at things from the worldly point of view — the flesh and blood inspiration that is still *avidya*. The veil of ignorance prevented him from seeing as the Spirit sees things. Jesus could have said to him again: "Begone Satan" (as in Mark 8:33). But instead he tries to explain to him: "If I do not wash you, you can have nothing in common with me" (v. 8). Peter would be cutting himself off from his Lord and from all share in his ministry and in his glory because he did not appreciate his Master's outlook."[10] Peter has yet to learn to accept the total mystery of self-emptying — unto love and service even of one's betrayers. For Jesus would also wash Judas' feet and love him "unto the end," even though He knew that very soon he would betray Him. Our Lord's answer to Peter's protest shows that his act was not meant to be only a lesson in Christian humility, but of the disciples' incorporation into him "so that they too are brought to share in their triumphant humiliation."[11]

It is only by surrendering oneself to the guru's action — however incongruous and baffling it may seem to the disciple — that one can learn to be happy and useful in his hands. It is only by letting God be and do — *laisser faire* — with and in oneself as He likes that one to become like Him. It is only by submitting to such a preposterous action as allowing God to be at one's feet, letting Him pour our his cleansing water on one's heart, that one can learn to be compassionate. It is only by allowing Him to abase Himself at a creature's feet that one can learn how to annihilate oneself in service at the feet of one's brothers. "Cleanse me of my guilt; purify me of my sin. Wash me and I will be made whiter than snow" (Ps. 50:2, 7). Only by such a cry from a broken and contrite heart can one be sure of God's incomprehensibly great mercy. "If your sins be as scarlet I shall make them white as snow," as he had promised us through Isaiah 1:18. Only so by total, uncomprehending submission and adoration can one really begin to see God in everyone who is at one's own feet in everything.

> He who with his heart to you surrendered
> Beholds forever You alone,
> And seeing all things as forms of Your love

Serves them as none other than the Self —
Triumphs, for he is immersed in You
Whose Being is pure Bliss.
So sang Ramana Maharishi to his Lord Arunachala.[12]

"Seeing all things as forms of your love, serve them as none other than
the Self!" For we are told, "Love your neighbor as yourself." Only
so, in the glory that shines within, can the Self-luminous One be seen
by us in each other.

Peter had yet to learn that there is no other way for the glory to
be revealed, "no other way to the abode." For he had not yet known
the *Satpurush* who is the *Mrtyunjaya*, the True Man who is the conqueror of death. Knowing Him meant knowing His ways and His royal
way of the Cross, which leads Him to "shine like the sun beyond
darkness" after his Resurrection.

I know this great Purush
Who shines like the sun beyond darkness.
Whom having known one crosses death.
There is no other road to the Abode.

                                          Svet. Up. 2.99

"Whom having known" — Only this true *Vidya, Brahma Vidya* can
lead us to "The Further Shore," wherein there is "no sorrow nor fear."
Peter mistook the symbol for the reality. "So we conclude that the
washing of the disciples' feet springs from and symboolizes the death
and resurrection of Jesus, which both effects the salvation of those whom
He loves, and binds them with Him in the same humble but victorious
destiny. By this death He goes to the Father; by their being made one
with Him in His death, the disciples, too, can "go to the Father and
inherit eternal life"[13] and perpetual Light.

The full significance of the meaning of this sign of foot-washing
would be made known to the Church only when he who had "crossed
death" by rising again would send the enlightenment of the Spirit (cf.
2:22; 12:16). John specifically recalls that "after Jesus had been
glorified," the disciples remembered, the disciples understood. But as
yet the Spirit had not yet been given fully. That is why Peter had been
protesting ignorantly as once before (cf. Mk. 8:32 f.). Then Jesus had

told him: "The way you think is not God's way, but man's." Now
He again patiently tells him: "At the moment you do not know what
I am doing, but later you will understand. If I do not wash you, you
can have nothing in common with me" (v. 7-8).

In typically Petrine fashion, the pendulum now swings to the other
end! From thinking himself too unworthy for Jesus to wash his feet,
he is now ready to let him wash his hands and his head as well! (v. 9)
Jesus answers: "No one who has taken a bath needs washing (except
for his feet); he is clean all over" (v. 10). Peter has understood Christ's
answer in verse 8 superficially, as if a new rite of purification were
being instituted. Jesus replies that his sacrifice has already achieved
this purification. (Cf. 15:2-3; 1 Jn. 1:7; Heb. 10:22.)

8. Overflowing of the waters

There can be no quantitative measurement of the effectiveness of
what Christ has done for His loved ones — including Judas. So he adds,
"And you are clean, but not all" (v. 11). There is no end to His love
and mercy — for all; like the sun that shines without distinction on the
good and the evil is His overflowing generosity, and like the waters
He pours out on the earth.

You visit the earth and water it and make it overflow.
You load it with riches.
God's rivers brim with water to provide their grain.
This is how you provide it;
by drenching its furrows, by levelling its ridges,
by softening it with showers, by blessing the first fruits,
You crown the year with your bounty,
Abundance flowers wherever you pass,
The desert pastures overflow,
the hill-sides are wrapped in joy,
the meadows are dressed in flocks,
the valleys are clothed in wheat.
What shouts of joy, what singing!

Psalm 65:9-13

You visit the earth and water it and make it overflow! This indeed is what God did when He visited our earth in the form of His Son Jesus. He made it overflow with his humble compassion. Jesus at the feet of His disciples washing their dust and stains away is perhaps one of the most deeply moving, revolutionary, novel, and typically "Christian" scenes in the history of religious literature. And again water is the instrument He chooses to use.

9. The significance of the action clarified

"When Jesus had washed their feet and put on his clothes again, he went back to the table. 'Do you understand,' he said, 'what I have done to you? You call me Master and Lord and rightly, so I am. If I then, the Lord and Master, have washed your feet, you should wash each other's feet. I have given you an example so that you may copy what I have done to you" (v. 12-15).

Our Lord Himself thus clarifies the significance of His action. He does not for a moment hesitate to acknowledge that He is their guru, but as He proceeds to say, "No servant is greater than his master, no messenger greater than the man who sent him" (v. 16; cf. Matt. 10:24). It was not simply that Jesus was observing civil customs. Guests going out to dinner were expected to bathe so that on arrival their hosts had only to remove the dust off their feet. But Jesus actually did much more than slight removal of dust after the real dust had been removed in the total bath. Jesus shows them that the action which the feet-washing portrays is actually a complete bath — beyond which no further cleansing is required. As a point of practical application, the meaning of this action is made abundantly clear. Not only do his disciples share in the fruits of Jesus' life work; they must also imitate its spirit. "You too have the obligation to wash one another's feet." It is their duty to practice the humility signified by this act.[14] And yet how very difficult it is for us and for the best of Christians to imitate Christ's staggering humility in practice!

10. Jesus the Karma-Yogi

"If you know these things — blessed are you if you do them" (v. 17). This is the ninth "beatitude" Christ promises us. It is only in doing, not theorizing, that we prove our love. "An ounce of practice is better than a pound of theory," Swami Sivananda used to say. If love means anything, it is essentially a giving of self and a doing away with self. Whatever true love gives, or does, it gives or does not for itself, for its own gratification. "Greater love than this no man hath, than that he lay down his life for his friends," Jesus was to tell his disciples in the last discourse that followed the washing of their feet (15:13). And he showed them this beforehand in the symbolic action of foot-washing. He warned them, too: "I am not speaking of all of you; I know the ones I have chosen; but what Scripture says must be fulfilled: Someone who shares my table rebels against me." I tell you this now, before it happens...so that when it does happen, you may believe that...I am He" (v. 18-19).

This is indeed *Nishkam karma*, selfless service taught in the Gita but going further — even unto giving up one's life for one's betrayer. This is work and service as sacrifice par excellence (B. Gita 3.9), without attachment and for *loka-sangraha* — the welfare of the world (B. Gita 3.25). Serving and working "free from desire and egoism," this indeed is bliss and beatitude and the secret of it. "Not those who say, 'Lord, Lord,' but those who do the will of my Father will enter the Kingdom of Heaven" (Matt. 7:21). So also one reads in the Gita" "Those who follow not my doctrine (who slight my teaching) and do not follow it...are men blind to wisdom, confused in mind; they are lost" (3:32). There is no greater example, perhaps, of the Gita's teaching on karma yoga than Jesus' washing of his disciples' feet, and especially those of Judas. The great teaching of the Gita is precisely this ascesis of action. Act and work one must — but not for one's own profit and satisfaction.

"Not by refraining from action does man attain freedom from action. Not by mere renunciation does he attain supreme perfection. But great is the man who, free from attachments, and with a mind ruling with powers in harmony, works on the path of karma yoga, the path of consecrated action" (B. Gita 3.4-7).

Jesus was then the great karma Yogi — seeking nothing for Himself but only the imitation and glory of His Father; never man's honor or good pleasure, and he worked ceaselessly and sought no honor. What honor did he find in the action of foot washing? "My Father goes on working and so do I," he said to those who were scandalized because he "worked" a miracle on the Sabbath day (Jn. 5:17; cf. Jn. 5:30, 34, 36, 41-44). "When a man's doctrine is his own, he is hoping to get honor for himself; but when he is working for the honor of him who sent him, then he is sincere" (Jn. 7:18). This he said to the Jews who wanted Him to show off His works. "Let your disciples see the works you are doing — you should let the whole world see" (Jn. 4:7). But Jesus did his works only for the glory and love of His Father and of men. His Father and men! These two were one passion for Him. For Jesus to speak of love and actually loving were the same things, as to love the Father and to love men was the same thing.

11. "Serve, love, give"

"The words of Jesus were vital and aflame. They burned themselves into the depths of the very consciousness of his hearers. And the reason for this? When Jesus spoke, His blessed words came from the depths of a limitless love and an infinite, divine compassion that thrilled with an all-consuming and powerful desire to do good to men, to serve, to help, to save. This compassion to purify, to raise and to save mankind verily constitutes the sacred heart of Jesus."[15]

Thus spoke a Hindu sage who himself gave to his disciples the motto: "Serve, Love, Give, Purify, Meditate, Realize." It is only by selfless service, that is service or work [karma], in and through which one seeks nothing for oneself, neither success nor praise nor gain nor satisfaction (an extremely difficult yoga indeed) but simply to help another that one learns the meaning of true love; and that loving means giving. Only thus can the heart become purified enough to keep still for meditation.

Only then can one, through *dhyan* — which is "the unceasing flow of God consciousness" — attain to Self-Realization.

12. "I am He" — "This indeed is That"

I tell you this now, before it happens, so that you may believe that I am He" (v. 19). Again the great name or title of Yahweh (Ex. 3:14) is used by Jesus; a Name and a phrase of the highest importance in the Gospel of St. John and of such significance to the *Vedantin*. "I, I am Yahweh... I am He from eternity... It is Yahweh who speaks... that men may know and believe me and understand that it is I" (Is. 43: 11, 13). Understand that it is I, that everything, everyone is only God, God's love, God's action "seeing all things as forms of your love." Not only does Jesus tell us that it is God who is washing our feet through Him, but that He is ever willing to wash everyone's feet, anyone's feet, for any and everyone is also God — with a name and a form. It is not easy to touch the feet of no matter what or whom, and to know that "This indeed is That" *Tad!* as the Upanishads put it.

John, too, for whom Mystery was irrevocably Incarnate — spoke in terms of "That." That something which we have seen with our eyes, which our hands have handled..." (1 Jn. 1:1) Doubtless this Person is That "which existed from the beginning, which was along with God, and Itself was God" (Jn. 1:1). Hence he who saw or received the Christ saw and received the God who sent him" (Jn. 5:18; 1:33; 16:30). He could say, "The Father is in Me and I in the Father" (Jn. 10:38; cf. 14:9-10; 17:21).

13. "Whoever welcomes me..." (Jn. 13:20)

And so, too, Jesus ends this tremendous symbolic gesture of foot-washing by the words: "Whoever... welcomes the one I send welcomes me, and whoever welcomes me welcomes the One who sent me" (Jn. 13:20).

Is it not at every moment that He sends us someone and in that someone His own Self? But we fail to recognize this Self and hence

we have sorrow and fear and delusion. But he "who sees all beings
in his own Self and his own Self in all beings, loses all fear. When
a sage sees this great Unity and his Self has become all beings, what
delusion and what sorrow can ever be near him?" (Is. Up. 6-7) Talking
of the true yogi, the Gita says: "He sees himself in the heart (self) of
all beings and he sees all beings in his heart (self). This is the vision
of the yogi of harmony, a vision which is ever one. And when he sees
Me in all and he sees all in Me, then I never leave him and he never
leaves Me. He who in this oneness of love, loves Me in whatever he
sees, wherever this man may live, in truth this man lives in Me" (B.
Gita 6.29-31). Jesus prayed for this oneness of love: "That they may
be One Thing — as we are One Thing."[16]

14. "By these gentle flowing waters"

To be "One Thing" with God is to be "one thing" with all men,
for He is the Self of all. In the light of the Hindu understanding of
Oneness in and of the Self, we could perhaps receive a new insight into
the first two commandments. Then Our Lord's words, "He who
welcomes you, welcomes me; he who welcomes Me welcomes the One
who sent Me" becomes luminous. For then we realize that in a sense
it is true that "No one is different from or other than myself" (N. Pa.
Up. 4.38). Then there is nothing to do but be like Jesus at the feet of
others. There is no possibility now of condemning others or of pointing
an accusing finger at others, for that would be condeming myself. Pilate
did not realize that when he condemned Jesus, he was condemning
himself; otherwise, instead of washing his hands and making a stream
to wash away his guilt, he would have instead washed the feet of others
and of Jesus, and know the answer to his question: "What is truth?"
Perhaps one could find no better way of concluding this reflection
on the waters that the Satguru Jesus poured over his disciples' feet than
by meditating on the first station of the Cross in the artist Jyoti Sahi's
poem and paintings on the Way of the Cross. He has painted Christ
standing before Pilate like a tree which has been condemned, and Pilate
appears like a rock, enclosed in a rounded shape. He points an accusing
finger at Christ. A stream at his feet reminds us of his act of washing
his hands.

He stood there, gnarled, contorted,
but flowering, like a "champa" tree
whose flowers are sold
in the market, as a temple offering.

The structures of man's idol worship
crouch heavy, perplexed, accusing,
like stones whose closed unyielding form
is rounded, eroded by the gentle flowing waters,
washing in their stream,
polishing into rolling rhythms
all that is hard and rigid.

By these waters the tree offers
its garlands of petals
accepting, rejoicing,
and at last breaking asunder
with its deep thrusting root
the hardness of earth.[17]

If the waters flowing from Pilate's condeming hands can produce
the champa tree, whose flower is used as a temple offering, what magnifi-
cent flowering trees would not grow from the waters streaming through
the gentle fingers of Jesus, "meek and humble of heart" — as they
cleanse and cool the tired, dirty and dust-laden feet of his
un-understanding disciples and bring them slowly to see how to love
God and one's neighbor as one's Self — by their willingness to die to
their little selves! For surely to do *Gurupad puja* is to say in effect:

Jesus, poor, humbled, crucified,
Who for love of me has died,
Let me die for love of Thee,
Let "me" die for Thee-in-Me?

CHAPTER NINE

Waters of Salvation

John 19:31-37

Jesus had begun his public ministry in the waters of the Jordan. He had used water several times for healing and purifying; he had worked "signs" through water. Now, as though to impress on us the beauty and significance of this lovely, lowly creature, he ordains that water be poured out from his pierced side, as he lies dead on the cross: water, the witness and proof of his death and, as it were, even a "legacy." John seems anxious to leave his readers in no doubt that Jesus is really and truly dead and that his death is within God's inscrutable but sure designs. Water is used to show this forth — in the record of "the great seventh sign," which includes both the death and resurrection of the Lord. Thus in John's Gospel water is seen constantly, till the end, as "something that stands for more than just the physical element: it is a term charged with subtle, spiritual meaning. Now it is the water of baptism, the entry into the supernatural life; now it is that very life itself, flowing like a fountain from the divine Saviour."[1]

1. The piercing of the side of Jesus

In order to prevent the bodies of the crucified from remaining on the cross on the Sabbath, which also, this year, happened to be the first day of the feast of unleavened bread, the Jews asked Pilate that the men's legs be broken, in order to hasten death, in time for removing their bodies before the Sabbath began. The law of Deuteronomy 21:22 f. forbade the body of an executed criminal, exposed to public obloquy, to remain beyond sunset. It was especially important that the bodies be removed and buried before the coming of the Sabbath, when such work could not be done. The Roman custom was to leave the bodies of criminals exposed indefinitely, and in any case a crucified person might linger for several days before death overtook him.[2]

For when they came to Jesus, they found that unlike the other two who had been crucified with him, he was already dead. His legs, therefore, did not need to be broken with a mallet. But to be sure that he was really dead (for evidently the death has occurred "too soon" for normal expectations [Pilate was surprised too], according to Mk. 15:44), a soldier pierced the side of Jesus with a spear and, according to the report of this eye witness, strongly emphasized at the point by John, blood and water issued from the wound. John seems to indicate that Jesus did not suffer the "passion"; there was nothing passive about Jesus' dying. (Even at the moment of death active verbs are used: "he bowed his head, he gave up his spirit" (v. 30). He actively and freely chose his moment and manner of death by crucifixion; he did not succumb to it. Not only that, even while dying he gave of His very Self. The last breath of Jesus was a token of the outpouring of the Spirit (cf. Jn. 1:33 f; 20:22) — symbolized and again accompanied by the presence of water.

2. Waters of life given by the triumphant Christ

"In his life Jesus had spoken of the waters of life that he would give. He had said of Himself: "From within him there shall flow rivers of living water." Now that he is glorified, raised upon the cross, the water that flowed from within permeated with the blood of his sacrifice, is truly the water of life, bringing salvation to men. The Spirit and the living water — these are the means of the re-birth by water and the Spirit that had been promised to Nicodemus."[3]

It is significant that He pours out this living water at the moment of his glorification. Consistent with His view of the Paschal Mystery, St. John, unlike the early Kerygma and the Synoptic Gospels, does not think in terms of Christ's glorification and Kingship beginning with his resurrection. It is already actualized in Christ's kenosis; Jesus' "exaltation" starts for John with His death, not with His resurrection.[4] For centuries Christians never pictured Christ on the cross except as a triumphant Christ. And it is in His moment of triuimph that He lets flow freely the waters of life and salvation.

3. Blood and water flowed out

This phenomenon can be explained medically.[5] The assertion that blood and water came out of the pierced side has received a good deal of medical attention, and opinion is divided among experts.[6] But John is far more interested in it as a "sign." The fact, as often in his Gospel, is subordinated to the assertion of some point of theological interpretation or meaning. He provides two clues as to what that might be from two Old Testament passages. One was an incident from Exodus (12:46 f.; Ps. 34:20) concerning the Passover Lamb, that its bones must not be broken. (Cf. 1 Cor. 5:7: "Christ our Paschal Lamb is sacrificed.") All this happened to fulfill the words of Scripture: "Not one bone of his will be broken" (v. 36). And again, an another place Scripture says: "They will look on the one whom they have pierced" (Zach. 12:10; cf. Num. 21:9; Rev. 17). God, it was prophesied, would pour out this Spirit on the house of David and the inhabitants of Jerusalem, that when they look on Him whom they have pierced, they shall mourn for Him as one mourns for an only child. Later we shall deal in greater detail with this second prophecy.

If these two texts are applied to the emphasized action of the soldier in (a) not breaking the legs of Jesus and (b) piercing His side, it becomes fairly clear what the evangelist is trying to state. In the case of the first prophecy, he is saying that Jesus Christ may be considered as the true Passover Lamb, slain at the proper time for Passover lambs to be slain, and like a proper lamb for the feast, without broken bones. In the case of the second prophecy, the evangelist is predicting that the Jews will come to mourn the death and the killing of Jesus, which is to say that he envisages the final triumph of Jesus in the conversion of the Jews.[7]

That the blood is mentioned along with the water is significant from several viewpoints. Cf. 1 Jn. 5:6 f., where the water, the blood, and the Spirit are mentioned as one. "From his fascination with the water theme, one might well argue the unity of the Johannine corpus. In Apoc. 22:17 we read: "Let him who thirsts come and receive the waters of life freely" and in Apoc. 1:15: "whose voice is like many waters.""[8]

In his Epistle, John tells us: "Jesus Christ is the one who came with the waters of his baptism and the blood of his death. He came not only with the water, but with both the water and the blood. And the Spirit himself testifies that this is true, because the Spirit is truth. There are three witnesses, the Spirit, the water and the blood; and all three give the same testimony" (1 Jn. 5:6-8). All three witnesses are present at the glorification of Jesus on the cross, and with Christ's death and the giving of the Spirit, already signified in verse 30 (bowing his head he gave up his spirit), the life-giving work of the Church begins, and hence the Church can be said in a sense to have been born from the wounded side of Christ.[9]

Water and blood (cf. Jn. 6:53-57) have been already well established as signs of salvation. John probably expected his readers to think specifically of the sacraments of Eucharist and Baptism, a common patristic interpretation.[10] Thus the blood shows that the lamb has truly been sacrificed for the salvation of the world (6:51); the water, symbol of the Spirit, shows that the sacrifice is a rich source of grace, and as we have mentioned, the Fathers saw, too, that the two sacraments, symbolized by blood and water, signified the Church, born like a second Eve from the side of another Adam (cf. Ephesians 5:23-32).[11] The famous and beautiful *Anima Christi* makes us pray:

"Blood of Christ, inebriate me. Water from the side of Christ,
wash me."

The Blood of Christ is the new wine of the Spirit that fills the
Apostles with virile Pentecostal courage. "The wine that germinates
virgins" and enthuses the lovers of Christ to lay down their own lives
as martyrs of the Church. But for the Blood of Christ to "inebriate"
us thus with His great love, there is alongside, flowing from the pierced
side of Christ, water — gushing forth plentifully first to cleanse and
purify the soul who would then be ready to be fired with Pentecostal
and burning love.

Speaking of these "twin streams of the life-giving sacraments,"
Marsh says: "It is quite plain that John is once more using a symbolic
element in what he takes to be an historical occasion, to drive home
a theological truth. John is engaged in a piece of antidocetic statement,
an assertion that the humanity of Jesus had been truly a physical
humanaity in the fullest sense. He had lived as a man, and had died
as a man. The Son of God had really come in the flesh. But His death
was not an event on its own, but one into which the other men could
enter through the sacraments of blood and water. So from the side of
Him who lived and died, there flowed the twin streams of the life-giving
sacraments of the Church in which Christ dwells."[12]

In his meditations on the Way of the Cross, Jyoti Sahi has painted
Christ crucified outside the city walls and St. John the Evangelist is
shown at the bottom corner of the painting prostrating, as it were, doing
his *pranam* before the "three witnesses" — the Spirit, the blood, and
the water. A stream from the side of Christ flows down to the Evangelist
— a very significant piece of artistic insight and theology. The poem
accompanying the painting reads:

> Like a waterfall pouring over the hot stone his limbs hang, white
> as bone. His body bent, flows into the ravine, where, in the dark,
> a lonely prophet throws himself beneath the stream, thirsty, longing
> for the cool spirit with white wings, descending as clear water
> springs. Moses struck the sheer face of rock with his rod, releasing
> from its closed heart a fountain cool and life-giving in that burning
> place. . . [13]

4. The crucifixion — a process of "opening"

> Releasing from the closed heart a fountain, cool and life-giving
> in that burning place...

The heart of Christ was the "burning place," burning with love of the Father and of men. It was pierced open with the lance of the soldier, as Moses had struck open the rock with his rod. In this opening lay the door to the mystery of the Eternal. Christ said, "I am the door" (Jn. 10:7, 9). The whole of Christian life became "a journey in the Spirit through Christ to the Father."[14] It is on the cross above all that Jesus teaches us the secret of the open door, into the mystery of silence that is the Father, beyond all name and form. His wide-open arms and wide-open heart make the event of the crucifixion "a process of opening, in which the scattered man-nomads are drawn into the embrace of Jesus Christ, into the wide span of his outstretched arms, in order ot arrive in this union, at their goal, the goal of humanity... And once again it becomes clear that Chirst is the completely open man in whom the dividing walls of existence are torn down, who is all, "Transition" (Passover, *Pasch*).[15] "The door of the true is covered with a golden disc. Open that, O Pushan, that we may see the nature of the True" (Isa. Up. 15). One might say Christ is the "Through" to God. It is interesting, incidentally, that the word for "door" in Hindi is *dwar* and the word for "through" *dwara*; and that the place of pilgrimage through which thousands pass each year to the Himalayas, is called *Haridwar*: the gate of God. In the light of all this, the liturgical prayer-ending so often on our lips, "Through Christ our Lord," might become more meaningful. He is the "through whom" and the mystery of the Cross and Easter become a mystery of transition. He is the true *Haridwar*.

For John, the picture of the pierced-open side forms the climax not only of the Crucifixion scene but of the whole story of Jesus. Now, after the lance trust that ends His earthly life, His existence is completely open; now He is entirely "for," now He is truly no longer a

single individual, but "Adam" (*admi* in Hindi means man), from whose
side Eve, a new mankind, is formed. . . The story of Gen. 2:21 f. seems
to be echoed here in the recurrence of the word *side* (usuallly translated
"rib"). The opened side of the new Adam repeats the creative mystery
of the "open side" of man: it is the beginning of a new definitive community of men with one another, a community symbolized here by water
and blood, in which John points to the basic Christian sacraments of
baptism and Eucharist and through them, to the Church as the sign of
the new community of men.

"The fully opened Christ, who complete the transformation of being
into reception and transmission, is thus visible as what at the deepest
level he always was: as 'Son.' So Jesus on the Cross has truly entered
on 'his' hour, as once again John says. This enigmatic mode of speech
may now perhaps become to some extent comprehensible. . . For to
be the man for others, the man who is opened and who thereby opens
up a new beginning, means being the man in the sacrifice, sacrificed
man (the true *Purush*). The future of man hangs on the cross. And he
can truly come to himself by letting the walls of his existence be broken
down, by following him who as the pierced and open one has opened
the path into the future."[16]

5. One-ing and conformity

It now becomes more clear why it is the cross tht gives hope for
the future of man and why the cross forms the center of Johannine
theology. One recalls Our Lord's words: "And I, if I am lifted up from
the earth, will draw all men to myself" (Jn. 12:32). This sentence is
intended to explain the meaning of Jesus' death on the cross and the
direction in which the whole of John's Gospel is intended to point[17]
— viz. to oneness and unity.

It is only through entering this door, then, that one finds the Way
(for "the Door" is also "the Way") to the Father; who is "the end
of our love-longing" — *Tadvaanam* (Kena Up. 4.6) — where alone
all our longings and loves are totally satisfied because we are "oned"
to Him;; we are not-two; we find, and are, our true Self.

We are so both and oneful
Night cannot be so sky
Sky cannot be so sunful
I am, through you, so I.

These lines of E.E. Cummings written in another context can become meaningful and enable us to see how Johannine *Advaita* points in the same direction. It is only through "the pierced and open one" that it is possible for man to know Oneness in its total reality. "He who is in the sun and in the fire and in the heart of man is One. He who knows this is one with the One" (Maitri Up. 6:17) and because He is one, He is our bridge to Eternity — if we take refuge in this pierced open heart.

> I go for refuge to God who is One in the silence of eternity, pure
> radiance of beauty and perfection in whom we find our peace. He
> is the bridge supreme which leads to immortality.
>
> Svetasvatara Up. 6:19

Looking at Christ crucified, some of these Upanishadic texts become more meaningful and at the same time render the Christ-heart more luminous.

It is only by entering in through this Open Door that one becomes *like* Christ — conformed to Him *sarupya*. There are four degrees of union: (i) *salokya* — being in/of the same world: those who "leaving him, fled" were not of the same *lok* as Christ; (ii) *samipya* — coming near (as did those who cared enough to approach the cross and the crucified One), those who lingered nearby; (iii) *sarupya* — those who approaching close become like unto Him; and (iv) *sayujya* — those who (having as it were, entered in) become united or one.[18] *Sarupya*, then, is being conformed. Our conformity to Christ is what our Christian life is all about. "The Word Incarnate took on himself the form of a slave, i.e., a life of toil and suffering, implying human death as part of our nature; these he assumed as the matter or rather the expression of his loving obedience to the Father. Thus he changed the meaning of Christian suffering and death. From mere consequences of sin, passively undergone as punishment, human suffering and death have become the material for our active openness to the mystery of Christ, the expression of our personal conformation with the Christ event. This supreme conformation with Christ in the depth of his kenosis results in conformation to his glorification."[19]

John consistently speaks, therefore, of the Crucifixion as part of Christ's glorification. This is surely a sign that he had understood "the mind of Christ": that he had grasped the meaning of the pierced open side. Had he not leaned on that heart and listened to its heartbeats? The Bible is full of the heart. "To approach God is to risk one's heart" (Jer. 30:21).

6. "That through the visible wound we may see the invisible wound of Love"

The spear that plunged into Jesus' side must have made a large opening, large enough at any rate, for Thomas to thrust his hand into the side of the Risen Jesus (Jn. 20:27). This wounded open heart of Christ whence flowed the living waters of the Spirit has been recognized from early Christian times, as we have seen, as signifying the mystic source of Church and sacraments. But the Fathers of the Church who show this clearly, basing their arguments on John 7:37-39; 19:34-37, move on from the wound in the side to the pierced heart. Perhaps this happened with the commentaries on the Canticle of Canticles 4:9. *Vulnerasti cor meum soror mea, sponsa* (Thou hast wounded my heart, my sister, my spouse).[20]

Certain elements of spirituality of the Sacred Heart can be found already in St. Anselm and Bernard, but it is only in the thirteenth century that it becomes clearly defined. The stigmatization of Francis of Assisi probably contributed to it. St. Bonaventure in the passage from the *De Vita Mystica*[21] invites us to enter into the heart of Jesus, that through the visible wound we may see the invisible wound of love, and give Him love for love, and turn away from sin, which caused the wound. From this time on, devotion to the heart of Jesus flourished in the world of mystics who, one could perhaps say, tend to read the Scriptures the *Dhvani* way (cf. Introduction), going beyond the literal or implied meaning to the depth meaning, which they can see with the eyes of the heart. Thus, to mention only a few remarkable mystics of the pierced heart, there were the Cistercian nuns of Helfta, Gertrude and Mechtilde; the Italina Franciscans, Bernardine of Siena, Angela of Foligno; the Dominicans, Catherine of Siena in Italy, Suso and Tauler in Germany; the Carthusians, Ludolf and Lanspergious, who were instrumental in having the devotion adopted by the whole order. In the fifteenth century it took the more ascetic form, with clear-cut exercises for achieving union with the heart of Jesus. In the Society of Jesus, though it was not explicit in the origin of the order, it developed through the prayer *Anima Christi*, through Favre, Nadal, Peter Canisius, Borgia, until the seventeenth century, when it became part of Jesuit spirituality. It developed further through the "Berullian itinerary" that brought the soul to a deep conformity with the mystery of the Incarnation-Redemption (Phil. 12:8 Exinanivit), Fathers de Condrena d Ilier, and finally St. Margaret Mary of the Visitation Order, who made the devotion popularly known through the revelations she received. The founder of the visitation, Francis de Sales had already written to Jane Francis de Chantal in 1611: "Our little congregation is the work of the Hearts of Jesus and Mary. The dying Saviour gave us birth through the piercing of his Sacred Heart." After this there is what the second Nocturne of the Office calls the triumphant progress of the cult of the Sacred Heart. Gradually, it is no longer the scene on Calvary and the lance piercing the side of Christ, but His Heart which is taken as the symbolic focus of the person. The heart stands for the person; the term *Sacred Heart* becomes a Name for Christ, and the Risen Glorious Christ retains forever the mark of the wounds (cf. Apoc. 5:6). Thus the hymn of Vespers for the feast says:

> *Tu nostra terge vulnera*
> *Ex te fluente sanguine*
> *Tu da novum cor omnibus*
> *Qui Te gementes invocant.*

(You staunch our wounds with the blood that flows from your side; you give to all who sigh to you a new heart.)

By the end of the eighteenth century there were many institutions consecrated to the Sacred Heart — right through the nineteenth century up to the sixties and seventies of our own century, when the Sacred

Heart devotion began to be looked upon by some with disfavor and criticism as soft and sentimental, perhaps not without some reason. The Church in India — and probably in the East on the whole — remained largely untouched by this "wave" of hypercritical attitude.

7. The heart in the biblilcal and Indian traditions

The heart plays a vital role and is given great importance in the Bible (an Oriental book) as in India. The heart is the place wehere man meets God, an encounter which becomes fully effective in the human heart of the Son of God. In Hebrew the heart is much more than the affective life. It stands for the "inside" of the man; it includes his memory, ideas, plans, decisions, thoughts. "To approach God is to risk one's heart" (Jer. 30:21). Before God, man realizes that he is called into question to the very depths of his being (Heb. 4:16). God knows the "stubborn and rebellious heart" (Jer. 5:23), "the uncircumcised and deceitful heart" (Lev. 26:41; Hos. 10:2). Just as Christ's heart was pierced, so must man rend his heart (Jer. 12:13) and present himself at God's feet "with a broken and contrite heart" (Ps. 51:17). Then "He creates in us a clean heart" (Ps. 51:12), for "the thoughts of his heart are from age to age" (Ps. 33:11). Paul's great prayer that "Christ may live by faith in your hearts" (Eph. 3:17) leads into and links with the Indian spiritual tradition about seeking the Transcendent God "of the highest heavens" within the heart where he abides as the Immanent One.

The heart in the Hindu tradition has also always played a great role and had a deep appeal — not only in the popular religion (Hanuman had *Rama* written in his heart, which he tore open), but also in the Vedantic tradition which speaks of the interiority of "the cave of the heart," "the space of the heart," "the lotus in the heart," "the inner space," etc. (cf. Chandogya Up. 8.l; Katha Up. 2.12.20, 5.12; Mundaka Up. 2.1, 10, 3.1.7;; Taittiriya Up. 2.1, etc.).

"He who knows all and sees all, and whose glory the universe shows, dwells as the spirit of the divine city of Brahman in the region of the human heart... In the supreme golden chamber is Brahman, indivisible and pure. He is the radiant light of all lights and this knows he who knows Brahman'' (Mundaka Up. 2.2.7 & 9).

That God is to be found hidden, hidden in the heart of every being as the *Antaryami*, the indwelling, controlling Spirit, is a constantly found theme in Indian spiritual tradition. And it is therefore a fairly safe hazard to say (and based also on my personal experience of dialogue with Hindu friends, artists and spiritual guides) — that devotion to the heart of Christ makes eminent sense and has a powerful appeal to the Indian spirit. And the streams of living water that come gushing from the rock-cave of the heart might be understood as the true Ganga Mata — the pure water that springs from the source, plentifully and unceasingly.

> Ceaselessly they flow from the depths, pure, never sleeping, the Ocean their sponsor; following the channels ordained by the Thunderer Now may these great divine waters quicken me! Waters may pour from heaven or run along channels dug out by men; or flow clear and pure having the Ocean as their goal. Now may these great divine waters quicken me!
>
> Rig Ved. VII 49.1-2

Ceaselessly, too, the divine purifying waters flow from the depths and through the channels men have dug out in the form of the Wound, for have we not pierced it with the lance of our sin and insensitivity to God's Word of Love? They flow pure and clear, cleansing and refreshing the hearts of men who draw near enough to look at Him whom they have pierced.

8. "They shall look upon Him whom they have pierced" (Jn. 19:37)

To relish this word of "the waters flowing from the pierced open heart of Christ," one has to sit and to gaze; a deep and long contemplation; a gazing that is transforming; a looking that is "one-ing"; a sitting that is a moving in, "entering within" into "the invisible wound of love." And before entering this place of *darshan* or "show-ing," as Juliana of Norwich would say, one has naturally first to remove one's shoes, for the ground on which we stand is holy. The door through which we wish to enter in is the door to the Holy of Holies.

There are various ways of looking "on Him whom they have pierced." Some passers-by looked on Him and were curious; others looking may have been struck by something of the beauty and serenity of the Face of Innocence — "the most beautiful of the sons of men" — now disfigured and treated as "a worm and no man" (cf. Is. 53:2-3). Others may have looked and paused for a moment, intrigued by one who seemed "harshly dealt with" but who seemed to "bear it humbly...never opening His mouth" (Is. 53:7), uttering no groans nor cursing, as others crucified might have done, yet they did not pause long enough to look, but passed on. They had other affairs, more important to attend to. They did not know "he was pierced through for our faults," they "thought of him as someone punished, struck by God and brought low" (Is. 53:5). Others might have suspected, as they looked, that here was someone perhaps different and maybe unique — "Letting himself be taken for a sinner, while he was bearing the faults of many and praying all the time for sinners" (Is. 53:12). Had they not, as they stopped to gaze on their way, suddenly heard him say, "Father forgive them, for they do not know what they are doing"? (Lk. 23:24) Others still paused to look, not to wonder or sympathize, but to jeer and mock. "He saved others, let Him save Himself" (Lk. 23:35). Even though many had heard Him speak and marveled that no one spoke as this man (Jn. 1:40), they had not "made His word their own," so they could not be disciples (Jn. 8:31); nothing He had said had penetrated into them (Jn. 8:37), so they "could not understand His language" (Jn. 8:43). Though seeing they had not seen, they could not see; even though they had looked on Him as He worked many miracles of healing, they had not looked on Him with their hearts; only with the critical eyes of the mind. But those who looked upon Him, the pierced One, with love, only a handful, and that mostly "the weaker sex" headed by Mary, the mother of Jesus, were found strong enough to stand and gaze with a heart full of the desire to understand the mysterious love of the heart of this man, so unlike all others. They looked on Him with love, with sympathy, being "in tune" with his heartbeat. They were of the "same world" *salokya* as He, having the same Spirit, and not the spirit fo the world. John brings out, from the beginning of his Gospel, the opposition between the Spirit of Christ and the spirit of the world. "He was in the world that had its being through Him, and the world did not know Him" (Jn. 1:10; 8:47; cf. Is. 50:2).

Those who looked on Him with love, began to suspect that they were looking upon the face of Truth, though "The face of truth remains hidden behind the circle of gold" (the golden disc) and prayed with the Upanishadic *rishi* (seer), "Unveil it, O God of light, and withdraw Thy blinding splendor, that I may behold thy radiant form" (Isa. Up. 15-16; Mascaro's translation). These two verses give us not only an insight into the dispositions of spirit with which one should desire to look upon Him but also help us to glimpse the wonderful prophetic Christian meaning. It is not possible to contemplate the glory of His face — "the glory that is His as the only Son of the Father, full of grace and truth" (Jn. 1:14) — without being drawn into the depths — awakening at last to oneself in the ultimate truth of one's being, in the eternal nonduality of that glory. Abhishiktananda, speaking of the "Johananine Upanishads" shows beautifully how the *rishi* whose "inner eye" had been opened, whose "inward eye of love" could see, could enter through the golden door. Man cannot force this entrance. The door opens only from within, and in its opening, all his desires are fully and finally fulfilled.[22]

For there comes a stage in the contemplating, looking or gazing on Him when one is (a) transformed, and (b) can no longer gaze at all, for where one is "within" the Other, one cannot look at or upon the other.

a. Transformation

First the "seer" is transformed, for it is the property of beauty never to be gazed upon, without causing the beholder to reflect something of itself. No gazer or looker upon the Crucified and the pierced-open Heart could have been transformed more completely than Mary standing at the foot of the Cross. For her, "looking on Him whom they had pierced" was but the culmination of a life's gazing and contemplation on the face of Him who she had borne within her. *Sarupya!* — conformed to His shape of mind and form of heart. More than any other creature on earth — before or since, she gazed with her "third" eye of faith and love until she was able completely to "enter into" His heart. But one can only enter in if one has been first purified by the waters flowing from that opened side and received sufficient "inebriation" from all that is not God. *"On n'entre que separe"* ("so

as to be free and separated''), wrote a French mystic of our own
century.[23]

One can only enter into the pierced-open heart if one's own heart
has likewise been pierced upon. God provides the pain that purifies and
prepares for vision and the ''one-ing.'' It opens us up to the invading
torrent of His overwhelming grace and love. It enables us to see ''the
secret shining in all that is most dark'' in the cave of the heart.

b. Drawn within

For the final stage of this gazing is the being drawn within into
the depths of the cave of one's heart and awakening to one's deepest
self — in the ultimate reality of one's being. And having been drawn
into the deep, there is no one ''outside'' oneself; there is no ''other''
to gaze on and no one left to gaze. The unity and communion with the
Father which Jesus came to give us is now complete. ''No one has ever
seen God,'' He had said; now He makes it possible for us to see ''the
Ultimate and beyond brightness.'' He has enabled us to enter in through
the pierced opening because He is the ''only Son who is nearest to the
Father's heart who has made Him known'' (Jn. 1:18; cf. k10:30; 14:10;
17:21, 26).

9. "Darkness profound and brilliant"

Having entered into the dazzling darkness of the Father's heart
through the pierced-open heart of Christ, one can now be filled to the
full with the most beautiful splendor which He is — the *Svayamprakash*,
the Self that shines by its own light. ''There the sun shines not, nor
the moon nor the stars; lightnings shine not there and much less earthly
fire. From his light all these give light; and his radiance illumines all
creation,'' (Mundaka Up. 2.2.10). Similarly we read in Revelation
21:23: ''And the city did not need the sun or the moon for light, since
it was lit by the radiant glory of God and the Lamb was a lighted torch
for it.'' Significantly the sacrificial lamb, ''whose bones were not
broken'' and on whose ''pierced'' form they gazed, is mentioned with
the divine radiance.

> There all God's secret matters lie covered and hidden Under darkness both profound and brilliant, silent and wise. You make what is ultimate and beyond brightness Secretly to shine in all that is most dark. In your way, ever unseen and intangible, You fill to the full with most beautiful splendor those souls who close their eyes that they may see. And I, please, with love that goes on beyond mind, seek to gain such for myself through this prayer.[24]

This prayer of the Pseudo-Dionysius gives as clear and concrete directions as any yogic methods in the Upanishads, or the Gita as to how to attain experience of God-Realization. Only those "who close their eyes that they may see" — through *pratyahar* and *sarva-dwar bandh* — through control and closing of the doors of the senses, can be "filled to the full with most beautiful splendor."

10. "Filled to the full with most beautiful splendor"

In that light of "His infinite glory and through His Spirit" alone can we know "with all the saints and have the strength to grasp" — in that wide open wound of love — "the breadth and the length, the height and the depth, until knowing the love of Christ, which is beyond all knowledge, 'we' are filled with the utter fullness of God" (Eph. 3:17-20).

This love of God cannot be "grasped" (cf. Eph. 3:18, 19), but can be "known" by a mystic awareness of it through love (cf. Eph. 1:17 f.; 3:3 f.; Hos. 2:22 f.; Jn. 10:14 f.). This awareness is something deeper than scientific knowledge (cf. 1 Cor. 13), "love that goes to all that is beyond mind" — something that all our historical and form criticism can never give us but perhaps comes nearest to the *Dhvani* knowledge of India. It is more like knowing that one is loved by the other than knowing the other that one loves (cf. Gal. 4:9). Even awareness of this sort, however, can never grasp this kind of love.

It is only when the piercing of love has opened us up wide open enough like Christ on the Cross, that this *pleroma* or *Purnam* which is God can be ours. The opening *Shanti* path of the Isa Upanishad is perhaps one of the loveliest hymns in praise of the Pleroma which is Christ in God.

Fullness beyond, fullness here; Fullness springs forth from fullness.
And if Fullness is taken away, Fullness yet remains.

Christ, who is filled with the divine life transcendent, *Purnam adah* (Fullness beyond), fills us with it — *Purnam idam* (Fullness here; cf. Col. 2:9) and thus *Purnat purnam udachyate* (Fullness springs from Fullness). In this way a Christian can enter both the Church and the new cosmos which he helps to build and which is the fullness of the total Christ (cf. Eph. 2:23-23; 4:12-13; Col. 12:10 f.). Then if "Fullness be taken away from Fullness, Fullness yet remains" *(Purnasya purnam adaya, purnameva-avashishyate)*.

This is only made possible because out of the well of the pierced-open heart of Him who hung on the cross came, as He had promised, "streams of living water" (cf. Jn. 7:37-39). "I am the Alpha and the Omega, the beginning and the end. I will give water from the well of life free to anybody who is thirsty" (Rev. 21:6). Fresh drinking water, a symbol of life in the Old Testament, is to be a feature of the messianic age. In the New Testament as we have seen, it is the symbol of the Spirit. This living water of the Spirit is the legacy left by Christ dying on the cross for those who have the courage to love and desire life, to enter the pierced-open "cave of the heart" and be "hidden in his wounds." "But the legacy of cowards. . . is the second death in the burning lake" (Rev. 21:8).

Blood of Christ, inebriate me!
Water from the side of Christ wash me!
Passion of Christ, strengthen me.
O good Jesus, hear me. Within thy wounds hide me.

We need to pray this prayer "until in the ocean of They love we lose ourselves" (Keble).

CHAPTER TEN

Epilogue
Waters of Awakening

John 21:1-23

"I arose and I am still with you" (Ps. 139:18) — by the waters!
Even after His Resurrection, Jesus gives his *darshan* (his third manifestation, as John says in verse 4) to his disciples by the waters of a lake.
"When morning was come, Jesus stood on the shore." As to whether
this chapter twenty-one is considered an appendix or epilogue, whether
it is written by John to some disciple of his, scholars are not agreed.
But this beautiful and sensitively drawn scene of Jesus' "showing" his
tenderness and concern by appearing at the break of dawn and prepar-
ing a breakfast for them, would be as fitting a conclusion or epilogue
to this work as to John's Gospel.

1. "Epilogue and crown"

To say that this chapter is an indispensable part of the Gospel may
be more acceptable in the realm of theology than from historical

139

considerations. It is possible to hold that the Gospel would be seriously,
if almost indetectably, incomplete without chapter twenty-one. In spite
of stylistic differences and evident inconsistencies between this and earlier
chapters detected by biblical scholars, it is worthwhile asking, as Marsh
does, to what extent this chapter is a mere appendix or an essential
epilogue to the whole Gospel, much as the prologue is an essential
preface to the Gospel.[1] From 1:19 to 20:31 John gives his readers his
own profound version of the life of Jesus, drawing upon a rich tradition in such a way as to complement and theologically deepen the
Synoptic presentation of material from identical and similar sources.
But where Mark takes the story back to Hebrew prophets, Matthew
to Abraham, Luke to Adam, John takes it back to the creative action
of God Himself, in the word or purpose which established the world
and speaks of God's purpose and nature to man; His purpose and nature
being nothing but love. "God is love" (1 Jn. 4). So, too, at the end
of the Gospel, where Mark ends his story with the awesome wonder
of those who had heard that the Crucified one had been raised on the
third day; where Matthew speaks of a worldwide commission for a Lord
who would be with His people to the end of time; where Luke tells
of the final blessing of the Risen Lord as He parted from His disciples,
John portrays in his own characteristic and powerful symbolism how
the Risen Lord would find His disciples in their resumptior of life in
the secular world, and would there empower them to complete his
universal mission, in the mystery and power of that laying down of life
which has seemed to men the shame and defeat of the cross, but which
to the Lord and His community was the manifestation of the glory of
the eternal God. "Such a chapter is more than a mere appendix; it is
not less than epilogue and crown." And while one experiences the joy
of the Risen Lord, one begins, too, to understand a little of the meaning
of the loving Lord's *Leela*. How playfully He appears and hides; reveals
and questions; tries and confirms! He manifests His love with the
exquisite delicacy of a mother's heart — He cooked (v. 9-12); and with
the strong love of a father — He taught them fishing (v. 5-6). At the
end of such an Easter apparition, one could meaningfully sing the favorite
prayer of our Hindu brothers: *Tvameva Matach, Pita tvamev* (You are
our Mother, Father; You are our brother and friend; our wisdom and
wealth, our all).

Thus, "Whoever its literary author, the manuscript evidence indicated that 'this chapter' was a part of the Gospel from the beginning, that it is presumably from the time of the Gospel's publication subsequent to the death of the Evangelist. Concerning the canonicity and inspiration of the chapter there has never been any doubt. The reasons for the addition of this supplement will appear from the matters with which it deals."[2]

2. "I go a-fishing"

Peter's desire to go fishing thus expressed, received immediate response from his six companions. Whether it meant a return to their old profession or whether, as some think, it meant apostasy, they immediately agreed to accompany Peter. "They went out and got into the boat but caught nothing that night" (v. 3). Though night time was the best for fishing, it was, as it were, to show that without Jesus they oould not succeed even in doing what they wre previously competent at. It may have been also Jesus' way of teaching them yet another lesson — that it is precisely in the doing of a secular job, even if at at time of desertion or apostasy, that the Glorified Lord will make Himself known. This is the great link between the Christian of every age and the apostles who saw Christ in the flesh and in his body of glory.[3]

Too often one thinks that God can be encountered and should be sought only in prayer and in temples. Here Jesus shows that since his Resurrection he can be found absolutely anywhere and everywhere, in any job or situation. He is the Cosmic Lord, the Vishnu, the all-pervading One, the *Sarvatondmukhaya*, whose face is turned everywhere, the one who shines through any and every human face. "All this universe is in the glory of God, of Siva, the God of love. The heads and faces of men are his own and he is in the hearts of all" (Svetasvatra Up. 3.11). "See now the whole universe," as Krishna said to Arjuna: "With all things that move and move not, and whatever thy soul may yearn to see. See it all as one in me. But, he added, "Thou never can see me with these thy mortal eyes; I will give thee divine sight — *divya chakshu*. Behold my wonder and glory" (B. Gita 11:7-8). The disciple of the

Risen Lord can now see Him — not necessarily transfigured and radiant in glory, but nonetheless present, and under very normal, homely, and secular appearances and circumstances. "Where could I go to escape your spirit? Where could I flee from your presence?" (Ps. 139:7). He is to be found everywhere.

3. "As day was breaking"

"Just as day was breaking, Jesus stood on the beach, yet the disciples did not know that it was Jesus: (v. 4). Like all Resurrection narratives related in John 20 and the Synoptics, this story begins very early in the day. Jesus comes early. "The voice of Yahweh over multitudinous waters" (Ps. 29:3) is heard best in the early hours of the morning. Both the biblical and the Indian tradition assert it. The *Brahma-Muhrt* time before sunrise is considered the best for prayer and meditation. When all things are quiet around, when, after sleep, the mind is at peace, it is easier to listen to the Word of God, it is easier to recognize His coming — whether He comes in the majesty of His glory or "incognito." Then meditation becomes enjoyable and not a burden; a play rather than work as Acharya Rajneesh insists. One meets Him whom one loves, then "Meditation happens and your whole life will become a meditation, a celebration."[4] In the early hours of the day one is "awakened" to His presence; one is better able to "recognize" him. In the Resurrection apparitions one constantly meets with this phenomenon of unrecognition. They did not know it was Jesus.

Magdalene thought it was the gardener (Jn. 20:15). Something prevented the disciples on the road to Emmaus from "recognizing Him" (Lk. 24:16; cf. Lk. 24:30 f., 35, 37, 39-43; Jn. 16:20, 21:4, 6-7; Matt. 28:17). The Risen Lord's body, though the same body that died on the cross, was in a new condition; its outward appearance was changed (Mk. 16:12); it was exempt from the usual physical laws (Jn. 20:19; cf. 1 Cor. 15:44 f.). But when the heart and mind are relaxed after a night's good sleep, when one seeks the Lord at the break of day, the eyes of love can recognize and break through any "disguises" and say with the beloved disciple, "It is the Lord" (v. 7).

4. By the waters of the lake

While Jesus stood on the beach, he was unrecognized. The recognition came with obedience. As at Cana, the water was transformed into wine when the waiters did as Mary bade them: "Do whatever he tells you" (Jn. 2:5). So here, on hearing Jesus' command by the lake: "Throw the net out to starboard and you'll find something" (v. 6), they hauled in so many fish that they had to "drag the net to shore" (v. 11). Perhaps standing on the shore Jesus could see fish clearly. The 153 fish, however (whatever symbolislm one may see in the number, and many suggestions have been offered)[5], depicts again the extravagance and overflowing generosity of God's love. God does not calculate. Love means giving to the full and overflowing — like the abundant waters and gushing streams, like the overflowing river and the vast ocean. In Ezek. 47:9 f. it was promised, "Fish will be very plentiful, for wherever the water goes, it brings health, and life teems wherever the river flows." The image of the miraculous water flowing from the temple is seen to be conferring a marvellous fertility (cf. Jn. 4; Rev. 22:2). Love knows no limits; love knows how to recognize. Though John was the first to recognize, as usual it is Peter's impetuous love that makes him jump into the waters to reach His Lord; and one smiles to see that with true oriental courtesy, before jumping in, he does not forget to wrap "his cloak round him" (v. 7)! Had not Peter always been the first, the first with is protestations of love and loyalty and first also in insight (cf. Matt. 8:29, 9:5, 14:29) as well as the one perhaps who had failed beyond others (cf. Mark 8:32, 14:53, 14:66-72)?

By the time the rest of the disciples reach the shore and haul in the large and heavy-laden net, yet not broken (miraculously), there was no doubt in anyone's mind "that it was the Lord" (v. 12) who had already prepared their picnic breakfast on a charcoal fire. It was again bread and fish. Where had his fish come from? The same waters maybe? The way John describes his stepping forward ("took the bread and gave it to them") naturally recalls the Eucharist. It was as if the Lord wanted to celebrate this meal with them by the waters of the sea. Had not water been a witness to so many of the most important events of his life? And fishing in the waters now becomes a symbol of apostolic mission under Peter's direction.

For not only is water here the witness of Jesus' apparition after his resurrection and the recognition by his disciples, but also it is by this sea that Jesus gives Peter his commission and primacy. It is here that He concedes His own office of Shepherd to Peter: "Feed my lambs, feed my sheep" (v. 16-18). He gives Peter the chance to make up for his triple denial by three times asking him, "Dost thou love me?" The two Greek words used for "love" — *aagape* and *phileo* have led commentators to speculate on whether there was some special significance or whether John merely meant them to be synomyms. It is thought that the progression from the stronger word *agape* to the weaker *phileo* gives an intelligible reason for the use of two distinct meanings. Peter, now humbled, does not dare compare himself to the others, not think his love superior to theirs. His former self-confidence has gone. He has learned that his sufficience comes not from himself but from the Lord; he has realized that it is not being sure of his love for Christ that is important, but rather being certain of Christ's love for him that is to be the foundation and support of his life and his mission. And because Peter realized this (it was he who had denied, forsaken, run away and even tried to tempt and divert Jesus from the cross), the Lord chooses to give him the commission. It is not the perfection of the disciple He looks at, but his humility and love. "Lord, you know everything; you know that I care for you" (v. 17). "So at last Peter is brought to the point of being completely broken; and at that point he is completely remade in the recepiton anew of his divine commission: "Feed my sheep."[6]

Furthermore, it is by the waters of the lake, too, that Jesus tells the newly humble and strong Peter how in the future he will come to "drink the cup" that the Father had asked the Son to drink (Jn. 18:11; Mk. 10:38, 14:36); how he would follow the Good Shepherd in every detail while shepherding the flock confided to his care — even to laying down his life (Jn. 10:4; 11:27). Peter's crucifixion is the fulfillment of this warning of Jesus. This is the oldest written attestation to the tradition of Peter's martyrdom by crucifixion, an event well known to the Christians for whom this Gospel was written. Did Peter, on the road traditionally known as "Quo Vadis," on his way to his martyrdom, turn back in his mind perhaps to the waters of Tiberius where he had been told by Jesus how he would stretch out his hands and someone else put a belt round him, and take him where he would rather not go (v. 18)?

It was finally by these waters that John, "the disciple Jesus loved" (v. 20), heard Jesus tell Peter of his own future. When Peter, turning, asked Jesus: "What about him, Lord?" the answer was strong, if ambiguous. "If I want him to stay behind till I come, what does it matter to you? You are to follow me" (V. 22-23). It is not for us to know the day and the way our friends are to serve the Lord in the future; ours is but to follow the path Jesus shows us. John may be trying here to correct the current misunderstanding and question. "Did Jesus mean that the Evangelist would survive till the Parousia?" He points out that Jesus never said such a thing (v. 23). Did it perhaps mean that the beloved disciple would remain "abiding in Christ until his life's end"? For the Lord will not fail to come to his own, as the coming by the lakeside has shown.

One is reminded how John had "leaned on His breast at the supper" (vs. 20). This additional information, surely superfluous at this point of the Gospel, may indicate that the author had incorporated material from some independent tradition. The place at Jesus' side corresponds to the place of Jesus at the Father's side. Just as this place makes Him the revealer of the Father, so the beloved disciple's place makes him Jesus' revealer and exegete.[7] What did he reveal and explain? Only what he had long contemplated and finally become — Love.

Thus the beloved disciple lingered on, tradition tells us, to a ripe old age, teaching his disciples in turn only what love meant and how it was the sum and substance of the law of Christ. And his predilection for the waters probably lingered in his heart, too — the heart that burned with *agni* — the fire of love Jesus has come to cast upon the earth until the end — knowing, as he did, how Jesus Himself had chosen the waters to be His witness from the beginning of His ministry right up to His death and even after His Resurrection. Was it not His "great delight"?

> O waters, source of happiness,
> Pray give us vigor, so that we
> may contemplate the great delight *Brahman.*
> On your behalf we desire, O Waters,
> to assist the one to whose house you send us.

You, of our life and being the source.
Now I have come to seek the Waters.
Now we merge, mingling with the sap.
Come to me, *Agni*, rich in milk!
Come and endow me with your splendor!

Rig Ved. X.9.1, 3, 9.

"Now we merge" — "as I in you and you in me!" Had John learned from the waters how to merge into the ocean, the Source and the Goal that was his God? Had he learned from them the secret of the mystery of Christian Advaita?

5. An awakening

Last night, as I sat watching from my window in the Himalayan foothills, the Gangaji flow past serenely and swiftly (it was the last night of this, my book), what was my joyous surprise when I saw a large, saffron blaze just by her banks, but reflected in her as though the fire sprang from within the river! Was it "the Refulgent One," "the Radiant One," *"Agni"*, "the Son of the Waters who dwells in the waters," making clear to me the purpose of the living waters of the Spirit which Christ had come to offer? — that these purifying, cooling, living, thirst-slaking waters were meant to set us on fire, and that these waters, in turn, can only flow from the heart set on fire! Only "Out of his heart shall flow streams of living water," who is aflame with the ardor of Him who could say: "I have come to cast fire upon the earth and what will I but that it be enkindled?" — who has no other desire but this.

I invoke the true Gangaji that flows form His heart:

Fons vivus, Ignis caritas — Veni!
Da Nobis Pacem!
(O Living Fountain, Fire of Love, Come!
Give us Peace!)

OM SHANTI

Water in the Vedic Tradition

Introduction

Of all God's creations, water is perhaps the one which occupies a central, vital and very special place. This is true of it in all religious traditions. It is literally vital — for without it man cannot live in the physical sense, for fertility, abundance, joy, depend on water. One can easily say the same of it on the spiritual plane. "If any man thirsts," [and who does not?] "let him come to me and drink," said Jesus (Jn. 7:37). Man thirsts for a water that will slake his thirst forever — with total and lasting happiness. This water can only be given by God; God's grace, His life; and it can only be received through faith.

It would be interesting to study both in the Vedic and biblical traditions the place of water: how it is a precious and special creature of God and how the Master of the universe, who dispenses water according to His will, therefore holds the destinies of mankind in His hand; how water is the effect and sign of His blessing; how waters can be healing, soothing, purifying, life-giving, thirst-slaking, yet terrifying and destroying; how by the immersing into and emerging out of the waters man is symbolically and yet very really renewed; buried yet resurrected.

I propose to deal here with waters in the Vedas, and something of what the scriptures, the *puranas*, and the epics have to tell us about

147

the sacred Ganges in particular, and look more specifically at one
ceremonial rite using water — viz *Sandhya Vandanam*.

1. *Apas*

a. Waters in the Vedas

Waters and rivers in the Vedas are referred to with great reverence
as holy and deified. About twenty rivers in all are invoked (Rig Ved.
V.53.9; X.64.9; X.75.5-6). In Rig Ved. X.104.8, Indra is said to have
secured for gods and men ninety-nine flowing rivers. Rig Ved. X 64.8-9
speaks of rivers that are thrice seven, and the three great rivers —
Sarasvati, Saraya, and Sindhu — are called divine mothers. The river
Sarasvati has three hymns devoted to it (Rig Ved. VI.61; VII.95-96)
and many detached verses also. The Rig Vedic sages knew that the seven
rivers fell into the sea. These seven are held to be the Sindhu (Indus),
the five rivers of the Punjab and the Sarasvati. The latter, believed to
have disappeared in the sands in the Brahmana period — is now generally
identified with the modern Sarsuti, which is lost in the desert at Bhatnair.

The personification of *apas* (waters) in the Vedic hymns is only
incipient, hardly extending beyond the notion of their being mothers,
young wives and goddesses who bestow boons and come to the sacrifice.
They follow the path of the gods. Indra, armed with a bolt, dug out
a channel for them, and they never infringe his ordinances. They are
celestial as well as terrestrial, and the sea is their goal. They abide where
the gods dwell, in the seat of Mitra-Varuna, beside the sun. King Varuna
moves in their midst, looking down on the truth and falsehood of men.
They are mothers and, as such, produce *Agni*. . . They bestow remedies,
health, welath, strength, long life, and immortality. Their blessings and
aids are often implored and they are invited to seat themselves on the
sacrificial grass to receive the offering of the soma priest. They are
also often associated with honey. The celestial waters are identified with
the heavenly Soma, the beverage of Indra. A.A. Macdonell says that
the deification of waters is pre-Vedic, for they are invoked as *apo* in
the *avesta* also.[1]

Apas are addressed in four hymns as well as in a few scattered verses. From them we can see how waters, as in all religious traditions, are either uncreated or produced in a peculiar way. In the *Satpatha Brahmana* they are said to be produced out of *Vac*, the Word (VI.1.1.9; cf. Gen. 1:1-3). Panikkar points out that the pun that follows is also significant. The waters were set free, they pervaded everything [*ap*] and therefore they were called *apah* (water), and because they covered everything [*vr*], they were also called *vari* (water).[2] Water was the first element out of the first principle. The waters are the primeval element; everything else rests on them.

> For from the waters is this universe produced
> In the waters, O Lord, is your seat, that is,
> In the waters, O Lord, is your womb.
>
> S.B. VI.8.2:3-4

Speaking of Yahveh's "residence" in the ocean, and his "kingdom" in the waters, Philippe Raymond shows (p. 194; see Note 2) how Semitic literature often speaks of a predestined place in the heart of the waves which becomes *nombril du monde* ("the navel of the world"); i.e., the home or the sanctuary of the divinity. Yahveh puts his "throne" in the waters, "a high dwelling" (cf. Ps. 4:3, 13; Gn. 9:6; Ezek. 28:2; Ps. 93:3; etc.) The mention of the creation of a temple in the waters (Jerusalem Bible says "you build your palace on the waters above") in Psalm 104:3 makes one think of the high dwelling of Mardull in poems like Enuma-elish VI and other extra-biblical texts — though some may be poets of the Old Testament period. And again, "of this universe, it is in truth the waters that were made first. Hence when the waters flow, then everything here, whatsoever exists, is produced" (S.B. VII 4.1.6). "The Waters are the foundation of all this Universe" (S.B. XII 5.2.14).

"The Waters are the foundation of all this Universe" (S.B. XII 5.2.14).

These short sentences taken from longer passages show the primordial status given in the Vedas as in other cosmologies to the waters rather than to any other element. Waters are the basis and foundation of the universe. In everyday Hindu life even today, it is a common practice to immerse used things, utensils, *murtis* (idols or images) in sacred rivers. Deceased children and holy men are returned to the earth or to the waters. They are not cremated.[3] All this symbolizes the same thing: the return to the origins. (It would be interesting to see similarities in the biblical traditon, such as the one already referred to above both for the cosmologies and the origin of the universe.)

2. The deification of waters

The deity is celebrated in the *Apan Napat* hymn (Rig Ved. II.35). Verse 9 reads: "He, the Son of waters, of color unfading, performs his work within the body of another." Or, as another translation has it: "The Son of waters has occupied the lap of the prone (waters) himself upright, clothing himself in lightning. Bearing his highest greatness, golden-lined, the swift streams flow around [him].[4] *"Hiranyarupah sah hiranyasamdrg apan Napat... Hiranyavarna"* (v. 10).

"The Son of waters is of golden form of golden aspect and golden line" because the Son of Waters is *Agni*. Fire is said to dwell in the water. Fire and water belong together.[5] The epithet *Asu-heman* ("swiftly speaking") is applied three times in this hymn to *Apan Napat*; in its only other occurrence it refers to *Agni*. Hence, says Macdonell, *Apan Napat* appears to represent the lightning form of *Agni*, which lurks in the cloud. For *Agni*, besides being directly called *Apan napat*, is also termed the "embryo" [*garbha*] "of the waters"; the third form of *Agni* is described as kindled in the waters.[6] Verse 10 speaks of the Son of waters "coming from a golden womb." The solar deity Savita is spoken of as distinctly golden (I.35) but *hiranya yonimay* [*hiranyagarbha* X. 121.1] at the creation] when Agni was produced from the waters (X.121.7).

Panikkar says, "At the sight of these waters we find prayer welling within us and in prayer become aware of the marvellous harmony of this universe."[7]

In the same Vedic hymn, *"Apam napat"*, we read: "The Son of waters, the Lord by the greatness of divine dominion, has created all beings... him, the pure, the shining Son of waters, the pure waters stand around" (V.2-3).

3. Waters belong to the three worlds

This is probably meant by the *tisro devite* — the three divine women "who desire to bestow food on the immovable god... he sucks the milk of them that first bring forth" (V. 5). *Agni* is spoken of as having three mothers [*trimata*] and three maidens of the waters [*yasanas tisro apyah*].

4. The waters possess also a certain intermediate character

This character could be described also from a cosmological point of view: They are neither air nor earth; they are on earth but come from heaven; they bring life but can also be lethal; they purify but can also be muddy; they flow on the surface but there are also internal rivers of water under the earth as well as in the individual.[8] The waters are neither solid like the earth nor intangible and gaseous like the air or the wind. They possess many of the features of solid matter and many also of the more spiritual elements. It is difficult to conceive of the spirit being unleashed from the earth, while air and ether possess no earthly properties at all. The waters, however, occupy an intermediate position and contain both the movement and life of the airy elements and the gravity and consistency of the solid; they are alive. They are lightsome, too, and glowing. Thus we read in the Mahanarayan Upanishad (1-2; 156):

> In the boundless waters in the center of the universe
> on the back of the firmament, greater than the great,
> having suffused with his splendor all the lights;
> The Lord of beings stirs within the womb...
> The cosmic waters flow. I am light!
> (The light glows. I am Brahman!)
> Now I have come to seek the waters,
> Now we merge, mingling with the sap.
> Come to me, *Agni*, rich in milk!
> Come and endow me with your splendor.

> Rig Ved. X.9.9

5. The waters

The waters possess an integral reality and thus they have purifying
and healing powers. Purification is their "first anthropocosmic function." The Rig Ved sings of these divine waters *apo. devih* (VII.49).

Unresting they flow, having their ocean as their chief from the midst
of the sea, purifying, for whom Indra the mighty one opened a path.

The waters that come from heaven or that flow in channels or that
arise spontaneously, that clear and purifying have the ocean as their
goal, set those waters, the goddesses help me here... How sweet are
the waters crystal clear and clearing... (v. 2-3) and in Rig Ved X.9
[*Urge dadhatana*]:

> You waters who rule over precious things
> and have supreme control of men
> we beg you, give us healing balm... (v. 5)

> O waters, stored with healing balm
> through which my body safe will be
> come, that I long may see the sun. (v. 7)

> Whatever sin is found in me
> whatever wrong I may have done,
> If I have lied or falsely sworn
> Waters, remove it far from me (v. 8).

6. Water as purifier

From very ancient times water has been regarded as a great purifier.
In the Rig Vedic hymns water is described as pure and purifying others
(VII 49.2 & 3) — "*Suchaya pavakah*". In X 9 hymns addressed to
waters invoke them to remove whatever sin or wrong one may have
committed: "Whatever is censurable and dirty" (Vajasneya-samhita
VI.17). In the same text the sage prays: "May the waters, our mother,
purify us."

In the Taittiriya Samhita, too, we read: "May the waters, the mother, purify us." Hail to you, divine, unfathomable, all-purifying waters! (I.2.1-2) We shall see later similar prayers used in the Sandhya Vandanam. Satapatha Brahmana states: "Water is a means of purification (I 7.4.17). Visvarupa (on Yagascneya I.191) quotes a long Vedic passage:" "Whatever creates doubt (whether it is pure or impure) should be touched with waters; then it becomes pure."

In the *Dharmasutras* it is laid down that water, hot or cold, can purify various kinds of vessels and ground. Articles of gold not smeared with "dirty things" (like remnants of eaten food) are believed to become pure by water alone; so, too, corals, shells, etc. found in water that are made of stone or silver on which no craftsmanship has been expended. Gold and silver sprang forth through the union of water and fire, so their purification is brought about best by their causes — by water, in case of slight pollution, and by fire in case of extreme pollution. [Cf. Lingapurana, purvadrha, 189-58). However, water — itself purifying — is at times considered impure. The water of flowing rivers is always considered pure. If water, originally pure, is kept standing one night or more, it should be thrown away. There is no taint in water that cannot be agitated by any living beings, and in the water of springs, that flow from the hills. Water of deep tanks, well, rivers, lakes — if it comes in contact with candalas and impure persons and things, should not be used. Vishnudharmasutra provides that water on roads which come in contact with lowest castes (like candalas), dogs, crows, buildings constructed with burned bricks, are purified by the wind glowing on them (V.Dh.S. 23.41). When a well, reservoir or dam is constructed by men of low castes, no *prayascitta* is prescribed for bathing in or drinking of that water though there are other occasions when performing *acamana*, sipping or touching water does purify. Thus it is laid down that "when a man engaged in any religious rites hears a mantra addressed to *pitrs* scratches his body, looks at a man of the lowest caste... speaks untruth, uses harsh language, has a fit of anger, touches a cat or a mouse, he should perform *acamana*.[9] (Rain water falling on the ground is supposed to be impure for ten days.)

It may seem strange to some that water, though purifying all sin, cannot purify certain evils, or that untruths, anger, harsh words should be put in the same category as touching a cat. Yet at a certain stage in Hinduism — as in other religions — "purity" itself came to be understood in a very impure, bigoted and narrow manner. One remembers, for instance, the Jewish custom of washing hands, feet, pots, and pans and how they got shocked that the disciples of Jesus did not wash before eating. Jesus then uttered His classic word on what purity and purifying are all about. Not what goes in through the mouth, but what comes out of his heart contaminates man. No wonder the Hindus through their many myths and legends believe that in the sacred Ganges "all their sins are washed away... and in reality they are" (Swami Shivananda).[10] One is also instantly reminded of the Christian belief in the purifying, baptismal waters in the Bible; of "baptism by water and the Spirit," which Jesus declared to be essential for entering the Kingdom of God (Jn. 3:5); the Spirit's primary function being that of cleansing and purifying, symbolized by water and fire. Thus there is in the Church's ancient hymn *Veni Sancte Spiritus* the verse:

> *Lava quod est sordidum,*
> *Riga quod est aridum,*
> *Sana quod est Saucium.*

> Wash what is sordid,
> Water what is dry,
> Cleanse what is filthy.

7. Waters also convey divine energy

Just as we would say today that blood is the conveyor of human life, we can say that waters also convey divine energy — but they are not the divine principle. Only God can control and rule them.

"What is more powerful, more self-confident, larger, and deeper than the fathomless ocean? What is more mysterious, more needed, more capricious, and more overwhelming than the rains, the vehicles of fertility"?[12] In Rig Ved V 83 there is the lovely song to *Parjanya*, the personification of Rain, the god of the waters from heaven:

> Invoke with this song the powerful, God-renowned *Parjanya*; win
> him by your worship like a bellowing bull; with quickening streams
> He deposits a seed of life in the plants.

He flattens the trees and smites the demons...
The winds burst forth, the lightnings flash,
The plants shoot up, the heavens stream,
the sap surges up in every stem
when *Parjanya* quickens the earth with his seed.
Gladden us, O storm gods, with rain from heaven;
may the Stallion emit his life-producing flow!
Bring here your thundering, pour forth your rain floods,
You are Divine, our heavenly Father!

Thunder and roar! Release the seed.
Circle in your chariot, heavy-laden with rain.
Tip downward your waterskin duly loosened.
Level the high places, fill in the hollows!

Draw the great vessel up, let it spill over,
Let the floodwaters burst forth and flow afar,
Saturate both heaven and earth with fatness;
Give to the cattle fair, thirst-quenching pools.

When, O *Parjanya*, roaring in fury
and thundering loudly you smite the wicked,
Thus the whole universe shouts for joy
And everything that is on earth rejoices.

You have poured down the rain; now withhold it, we pray you!
You have made the desert fit for travel
To serve as food you have made the plants flourish
Receive from us in return grateful praise! V. 1-10

8. Terrifying waters

As in the Bible, so in the Vedas we see that waters that are necessary
for life-healing, purifying, thirst-slaking, life-giving, are also capable
of destruction, are death-bringing and therefore can be terrifying. As
waters from the sea reflect demoniacal restlessness and the desolation
of Sheol by their bitterness, so here the rain must not be too heavy or
too prolonged or there will be risk of flooding out houses, fields, and
peoples. That is why *Parjanya* is begged to hold back the rains.

In India, as in Israel, man knows well what the blessings and curses of rain are. Every year we hear of one or another region of the country suffering from drought or perishing through too much rain. And man, with all his advanced technological knowledge, can neither bring forth rains nor stop them. As we read in Psalm 104, the mastery of God over waters is insuperable. It is only God who has created the waters on high (vs. 2) as well as those of the abyss (v. 6); it is He who rules the extent of their course (v. 7); who holds them back lest they submerge the earth (v. 9); who causes the springs to leap up (v. 10); and the rain to fall (v. 13); thanks to which prosperity is spread over the earth and the heart of man is gladdened (v. 11-18). One can, therefore, understand the negative attitude of men towards the ocean or the sea.[13] "The eternal silence of infinite spaces frightens me," said Pascal. The man of the Old Testament, too, according to his Hebraic cosmology, believing the ocean "surrounded by" the cosmos on all sides, was scared lest the waters, contrary to the God-established order, overstep their limits — in spite of Jeremiah 5:22-23: "I placed the sand as the boundary of the sea, a permanent boudnary that it cannot cross. The sea may toss but it cannot go beyond it; the waves may roar, but they cannot break through. But you people! You are stubborn and rebellious... even though I send the autumn rains and the spring rains and give you the harvest season each year."

Yet in the Vedas, the waters are "a resting place for all the gods" (Satapatha Brahmana XIV 3, 2, 13). They are prayed to as "source of happiness." "Pray give us vigor so that we may contemplate the great delight (Brahman) of our life, as being the source."

9. Water slakes thirst

In the Rig Vedic poem X.9, water is praised for slaking our thirst, bearing joy, and giving health.

> There waters be to us for drink
> divine are they for aid and joy.
> May they impart to us health and strength! V. 4

Now I have come to seek the waters
Now we merge, mingling with the sap.
Come to me, *Agni*, rich in milk!
Come and endow me with your splendor! V. 9

Both these verses have their resonance in the Bible. We remember Jesus'
declaration: "He that believes in me shall never thirst" (Jn. 6:35) and
"If any man thirst, let him come to me and drink" (Jn. 7:37) and the
Book of Revelation 22:17: "Let the thirsty one come — anyone who
wants to, let him come and drink the water of life without charge."
This just about sums up the graciousness, liberality, and availability
of "Sister Water."

One may fittingly end with St. Francis of Assisi's prayer in his
canticle to the sun:

Be praised, my Lord, for Sister Water!
For greatly useful, lowly, precious, chaste is She!

Whether she falls gently or powerfully bathes the dry earth in the form
of rain, or is stored up in wells or tanks, whether she leaps and bounds
over hills and valleys as streams and springs, or whether she flows swiftly
or peacefully as a river to the ocean, her source and her goal — water
is as much a teacher and a reminder to man of his own course and goal
as she is to him a source of life. She makes it possible — if he bows
low enough to drink of her or bathe in her — to be renewed, to be reborn,
until "streams of living water flow forth from his heart."

APPENDIX II

The Sacred Ganges

I am the Ganges among the rivers.

(Bhagavad Gita X.3)

Though all rivers in India are considered holy, the most sacred of all rivers is the Ganges, lovingly called *Gangamata* by the devout Hindu. It may be of interest to know the mythological origin and importance of the Ganges, from which comes the sacredness attached to its waters even today. But first let us see *what* the Ganges means to the Hindus and then *why*.

1. What the Ganges means to the Hindus

Every Hindu longs for a dip in her. If he cannot obtain the grace to die at her banks, he longs for a drop of her waters and prays that his ashes will be laid to rest in them. Thousands of pilgrims coming to Haridwar and Rishikesh each year take back *Gangajal* in a sealed *lota* (vessel) to their homes or to their less privileged friends. When crossing the holy river in a ferry at Rishikesh, for instance, they will first sing out her praises: "*Ganga — Mataki Jai*" and then put their hands out of the boat to drink a sip of the river. Whenever a religious Hindu takes his bath, he first invokes the Ganges and "feels her presence before he takes a plunge in the river." One can see hundreds of devout men and women having their daily baths or going down into these waters on certain occasions chanting mantras, invoking God to purify and heal them. *Sadhus*, *sanyasis*, and *sadhakas* desire to build their *kuttir* (huts or houses) by her banks to get the blessing of her *darshan* and to receive many lessons from her.

2. What lessons the Ganges teaches the discerning *sadhaka*

Anyone who has lived by the Gangaji will understand her teachings, her *maun vyakhya* (silent discourse). "The Ganges starts from Gangotri in the Himalayas, encounters many obstacles on her way, but finally reaches the goal — the ocean. Similarly, the spiritual aspirant should never give up the struggle, however insurmountable the obstacles on the path may appear to be."[1]

> When a little stream bursts from the earth it is full of life and energy, chatter and joy. And as it moves onwards, it meets obstacles and difficulties — rocks and twigs and stones all of which have to be embraced and carried along or else avoided. Until at last it has been slowed down and rests a deep, peaceful pool of still waters. And so our day should be. At the beginnning fresh and full of life and promises, as we live it through, the work, the difficulties and challenges of the day — so makes us run more slowly until as darkness comes, we lie a pool of silent water.

Thus wrote another modern lover of the Ganga, who dwells on her holy banks.

"The Ganges always gives you cool, pure water. It does not expect anything from you in return...always gives and asks for nothing in return. Expect nothing in return, not even appreciation or recognition. Both a rogue and a saint can drink the water of the Ganges, like the sun that sheds its light on the wicked and the virtuous. Develop equal vision like the Ganges..." So spoke Swami Shivananda of Rishikesh.[2]

One of the constant joys of watching Ganga water is to see her varied moods and colors; now green, now blue, now serene, now tumultuous. But always she sings her incessant "Om," reminding one of the Lord of the Waters, by those word she came into being, reminding one, too, of the necessity of constancy and *ekagrata*. Whether she is sprightly and sparklingly joyous or whether so still that she looks as though she were as static as a mirror, yet she flows on — she ever flows to her source, slowly, perhaps, at times, but ever surely. She is a real lesson in meditation which is "an unceasing flow of God-consciousness."

A description of the flowing Ganga, given in the Bala-kanda of the *Valmiki Ramayana*, will be recognized as very true by anyone, for instance, who has seen her meandering or leaping between Badrinath and Haridwar.

"The Ganges now flowed very swiftly, now tortuously, not it broadened out, now again narrowed down (when forcing its way through a ravine); now it was tossed high (when dashed against a rock) and now it glided. Now buffeted by the waves of the same water (when turned back by the wind), the water of the Ganga spouted upwards once more and dashed to the ground again" (Canto XI).

Modern saints and scholars still write ecstatically about her: "I bathe in the Ganga and swim in it. I adore Ganga and feed the fish in it. I wave lights before mother Ganga and pray to her. I do salutations to Ganga and sing her glory. I write about the grandeur and glory of Ganga. Ganga has nourished and comforted me. Ganga has taught me the truths of the Upanishads... To have a look at the Ganges in Rishikesh is soul-elevating. To sit for a few minutes on a block of stone by the side of the Ganges is a blessing. To stay for some months in Rishikesh on the banks of the Ganges and do *Anusthan* or *Purascharana* is great *Tapas*, which will take the aspirant to the abode of the Lord Hari. To live forever on the banks of the Ganges and spend one's life in meditation in Sivanandam. Mother Ganges bestows seen and unseen power on those who crave her grace. Sit alone on the banks of the Ganges. Concentrate. Meditate. Realize how spiritual vibrations accelerate your inner heart, even overriding your guilty conscience. Where has the supreme joy that fills you now all over, come from all of a sudden! How does she instantaneously withdraw your mind and conscience from the physical world to the regions of immortality, only to suckle you with bliss and blessedness! All glory be unto Mother Ganges, the giver of life, light of love, attain Brahman through her Grace.

When I am open to the wonder that the Ganga is, I am open to
God. The Ganga is a wonderful revelation of God's love and power.
The Ganga is a wonderful revelation of God's love and power. It is
He who rejoices our hearts through His lavish gift of the Ganga, He
who quenches our thirst through her sparkling waters. What would the
land be without the Ganga! Life can neither flourish nor even exist
without her. The believer sees the Ganga issuing from the bosom of
God. The river is not seen in isolation. What the Ganga does is what
God does. She is seen in God, and God is seen in her. She is bathed
in God's own glory. So to glorify the Ganga is to glorify God. To sing
her praises is to sing His praises. The Ganga is the ever-present, never-
exhausted, convincing assurance of God's infinite love."[3]

"The sight of the holy Ganges at night or at sunrise in Haridwar
or on the majestic ghats in Banaras surely empties our minds of meanness
and for the moment at least fills our hearts with a sense of nature's beauty
and with purity, and brings us in tune with the infinite," says P.V. Kane
in his otherwise prosaic and scholarly *History of Dharmashastra*. He
says, "Every Indian who is proud of the great religious and spiritual
heritage our country must make it a point to devote some part of his
time to frequenting holy mountains and rivers. . .as places of pilgrimage.
The number of people visiting holy places in the belief of accumulating
merit is sure to become less and less, as modern secular education
spreads. But it would be a calamity for the moral and spiritual greatness
of India if pilgrimages to holy mountains and rivers came to be stopped
altogether. . . Mountains and rivers! — The Himalayas and the Ganga
— "My father and my mother," as they have been called by a saint.
They are perhaps the two greatest and most glorious, the purest and
most purifying of *tirthas* (pilgrimage centers) in India. To most men
in India, great rivers like the Ganges and great mountains like the
Himalayas present a double aspect, viz. the physical aspect and the
spiritual aspect. A great river, apart from its volume of water, is deemed
to have a spiritual or divine life which animates it.[4] There are whole
separate treatises devoted to the glorification of the Ganges and the
pilgrimage to it, such as the Gangapattalaka of Ganesvara (1350 A.D.);
Gangavakyarali of Visvasadevi, queen of King Padmasimha of Mithila;
the Gangabhakti-tarangini of Gangapati; the Gangakrityaviveka of
Vardhaman.

Some of the holiest *tirthas* (pilgrimage centers) of India are situated
on the Ganga — Konkhal, Haridwar (originally called Gangadwar),

Prayaga and Kasi (Varanasi). This is another reason that the Ganges is invoked as the first among the many rivers invoked in the *Nadistuti* hymn of Rig Veda (X.75, 5-6). There are hundreds of verses in the Scriptures referring to the sanctity of the Ganges and eulogizing her purifying activity.

The *Vanapurva* (chapter 85) tells us: "In the *Krta* age all places were holy; in *Treta* age Puskara was the holiest place; in *Dvapara* Kurukshetra and in the *Kali* age the Ganges. The Ganges, when its name is uttered, purifies a sinner; when seen, it yields good fortune; when a bath is taken in it or its water is drunk, it sanctifies the family up to the seventh ancestor. As long as a particle of the bones of a man touches Ganges water, i.e., lies in it, so long does the man remain happy (or honored) in heaven. There is no holy place equal to the Ganges, there is no God higher than Kesava. That country and that penance grove where the Ganges flows should be known as the sacred spot of success (or perfection) since it attaches itself to the Ganges."

The *Anusasan* (26.26, 30-31) tells us: "Those districts and countries, those hermitages and mountains in the midst of which the Ganges flows are pre-eminent in *punya* (religious merit). Even those men who, after committing sinful acts in the first part ot their lives, resort afterwards to the Ganges, reach the highest world (or goal). That increase (in merit) which comes to men who bathe in the holy waters of the Ganges, and who then become pure in spirit, cannot be secured even by the performance of hundreds of solemn Vedic sacrifices" (39.30-31; 40.64.)

And again:

"If a person, after committing a hundred bad deeds, sprinkles himself with Ganges (water), the water burns, all of them as fire burns fuel" (Vanaparva, ch. 85).

The *Visnupurana* says, "The Ganges purifies all beings from day to day when its name is heard, when one desires to see it, when it is seen or touched or when its waters are drunk or when one plunges into it or when one takes (or sings) its name. When people utter the name of *Ganges*, even though living at a distance of hundreds of yojanas, their sins accumulated in three births are destroyed.

The *Bhavisyapurana* has a similar verse: "One becomes free from sin at once by seeing the Ganges or touching it or drinking its water and by uttering the name Ganga and also by remembering it." The *Maysya Purana, Kurma, Garuda*, and *Padma* remark that the Ganges is easy of access everywhere but difficult to reach at certain places — viz at Gangadvara (Haridwar), at Prayag and where it joins the sea; but that those who bathe therein, reach heaven and those who die there are not born again.

"The man, whether desiring it or not, who draws near the Ganges and dies (near it) secures heaven and does not see hell (Maysya Purana 107.4). No doubt the phrase "Whether desiring it or not" is meant to show the power of the Ganga-waters, rather as it is said that anyone who wittingly or unwittingly calls on the Name of the Lord is saved — because of the power of the Name. This would not take away from the truth that the strong and pure desire of the aspirant would surely make the deed even more effective. However, it may and does lead to superstitious beliefs and practices.

The *Kurmapurana* represents that the Ganges is equal to all the thirty-five million holy places declared by Vayu — in the heavens, in mid-region and on the earth, and that all of them are represented by the Ganges (I.398).

The *Padmapurana* asks: "What is the use of sacrifices rich in large wealth, what is the use of very difficult austerities when there is the Ganges honored easily and gracefully that yields heaven and moksha?" (I 477, V 60-59).

A similar verse in the Naradiya-purana says: "What is the use of Yoga with its eight *angas*, of austerities of solemn (Vedic) sacrifices? Residence on the Ganges is superior to all these" (38.38).

In the Varahapurana (chapter 82) the name *Ganga* is derived as *gam gata* ("that which has gone to the earth"). The Padmapurana (Srstikhanda 60.64-65) specifies the *mulamantra* about the Ganges as: *"Om namo Gangayai, Visvarupinyai Narayanyai namo namah"*. The Skandapurana, Kashikhanda (ch. 29, v. 17-168) contains one thousand names of the Ganga.

The *Padmapurana*, which holds that Vishnu represents all the gods and the Ganges represents Vishnu, eulogizes her as follows: "Sons abandon their fathers, wives their husbands, friends and relatives abandon a friend or relative if any one of these is adulterous or wicked or becomes *sandala* or kills his guru, or is full of all kinds of sins and hatreds; yet the Ganges does not forsake such persons'' (60.35). She is faithful with a love like Yahweh's in the Bible, for adulterous Israel who abandons Him.

It is now easy to understand why with so much devotion people seek to live by the Ganga, sip her waters, dip in them, bathe in them. She seems to be their purifier and friend, their mother and sustainer. Above all, it is the bath in the Ganges that is considered most important and salvific.

3. *Ganga-Snan*

The procedure of a bath in the Ganga is quite complicated and laid down with precision; e.g., the *prayascittatattva* contains a very elaborate *sankalpa*. The mode of bathing prescribed in the Matsyapurana 102 is common to people of all *varnas* and students of all the different recensions of the Veda.

Cleanliness of thought and body do not exist, it is believed, without a bath. Bathing is therefore prescribed for making the mind pure. A precise spot is chosen with the invocation to the Ganges: "You are sprung from the foot of Vishnu...save us from sins." A number of names of the Ganga (*Nandini* or joy-giving: *Amrita* or nectar, etc.) are to be pronounced while bathing. Holding his hands, the person casts water over his head a certain number of times with certain mantras. He invokes the clay, sips water *acamana* as prescribed, gets out of the river, and puts on two pure white garments. Then he performs *tarpana* for the satisfaction of the three worlds — when water is poured with both hands (unlike the offering thrown into the the fire in *sradha* — with one hand — wearing the sacred thread in a particular form, *upavita* — when satiating gods; in the *nivita* form when satiating men; after *acamana*, he draws the figure of a lotus before him, and offers on it *arghya* (respectful offering of water) — water mixed with red — sandalwood paste, flowers, and *aksatas* (grains of rice) — repeating the names of Surya, as *Bhaskar* (one who enlightens), as *Divakar* (maker of day), as *Prabhakar* (source of refulgence), etc. Having bowed to the sun and circumambulated three times (the drawn lotus representing the sun), touching a Brahmin, gold or a cow, the father should go to a temple of Vishnu — or as another reading has it, return to his own house.

In various scriptures and *puranas* one reads of this bath in the Ganges, which makes it clear why the *Ganga-snan* is practiced by thousands of people even today. Serious *sadhakas* living by this sacred river (or any other) will not easily miss their daily *snan*, even in wintry weather. We read, for instance, in the Balakanda of the Ramayana (Canto XXXV) of Viswamitra and party, including Sri Rama and Lakshmana, sighting "the Ganga, the foremost of all rivers, resorted to by the sages" and "all rejoicing to see the celebrated river whose waters confer merit (on those who resort to them) and which was frequented by swans and cranes" (7-8). Having then bathed in the river according to the Scriptural ordinance — i.e., after reciting a Vedic hymn known as the *Aghamarsana-Sukta* (Rig Veda X 98), duly propitiating the manes and gods (including rsis) with libations of waters, and also pouring oblations into the sacred fire. . . "the blessed rsis sat down with a cheerful mind surrounding the high-souled Viswamitra."[4]

Sri Rama then asks Viswamitra about the holy river Ganga, which "takes a threefold course (flowing as it does through heaven, the earth, and the subterranean regions). . . and how it meets the ocean — the ruler of rivers both big and small." Then, in answer to Rama's inquiry, Viswamitra expatiates on the origin of the Ganga in Canto XXV of the *Bala-kanda*.

4. The origin of the Ganga as given in Valmiki's Ramayana

Of the two daughters "matchless in beauty on earth" born of the great Himalaya, "the king of mountains," and his consort Mena, Ganga was the elder. Her hand was sought by all the gods of Himavan (the deity presiding over the Himalayas). "From consideration of piety (according to which the solicitation of a supplicant is not to be rejected) and out of solicitude for the welfare of the three worlds, Himavan gave his daughter Ganga, who is capable of purifying the world and who could carve her way (even through the air and subterranean regions) according to her own free will. Accepting the gift of Himavan in the interest of the three worlds, the gods taking the Ganga with them, left fully satisfied (v. 18). "She rose to heaven (the realm of the gods) in the form of Mandakini (the heavenly stream visible in the form of the milky way). She rose into the sky which allows moving space to all mobile beings. Last of all, she assumed the form of an earthly stream (as Ganga) capable of ridding the world of its sins (v. 22-23).

Before seeing what the Ramayana has to tell us further about how Bhagiratha practiced austerities for bringing down the Ganga to the terrestrial plane, let us see what some Puranic tales have to tell us about the birth of the Ganges.

5. Ganga's birth — as given in the Puranas

Once, in Mount Kailasa, Parvati closed the eyes of Lord Shiva with her hands. The sun, moon, and fire stopped their shining. This caused great havoc in the world which was all enveloped in darkness. When Shiva opened his third eye a bit, they bagan to shine again. Parvati, frightened at this, removed her hands and perspiration dropped from her fingers. The perspiration turned into ten Ganges with countless tributaries. These rivers caused havoc in the world till Brahma, Vishnu and Indra ran to Lord Shiva and requested him to avert this catastrophe. Shiva, feeling compassion, brought all the waters into one hair of his matted locks. The three then asked Shiva to give them a little water of the Ganges for their worlds. Thus Virajanadi began to flow in Vaikuntha, Manasa Tirtha in Satyaloka and Deva Ganga in Indra-Loka.

The Ganga thus came out of the supreme Being. She entered the feet of Lord Hari and reached Vaikuntha. She issued from Go-loka and passed through the regions of Vishnu, Brahama, Siva, Dhruva, Chandra, Surya, Tapa, Jana, and Maha, and reached Indra-Loka and flowed as Mandakini.

There is another story of how once Mahadev heard the music of Vishnu and his force melted into water. Brahma gathered this water in his *kamandalu* (vessel) and sent it towards the earthly region. This flow of water is known as Ganga. These mythological origins show again not only the power of divine music, but how in Ganga's origin, Brahma Vishnu and Shiva were actively involved; they show her divine origin, which explains, too, her power for purifying and healing men's bodies and souls.

Yet another story tells us how when Ganga married Lord Shiva and was about to leave her parents' house, her mother could not bear the separation. So she prayed that Ganga should be turned into a river and flow in the Himalayan region. Her prayer being granted, she was able to see Ganga every day.

That King Bhagiratha brought down the Ganges from Brahma-Lok to save the sixty thousand sons of Sagara is a story also found in the Ramayana (Canto XLII of the Bala-kanda).

The great King Sagara was one of the mighty monarchs of the solar race of which Rama was born. He performed a hundred *ashwamedha* sacrifices aspiring for Indrahood, kingship of the Devas. In the hundredth sacrifice, the sacrificial horse was stolen away by Indra for fear of being dethroned by the aspirant. Tied to a post, the horse was left within the premises of Rishi Kapila's ashram.

All the sons — (sixty thousand) of Sagara set out in search of the horse. As soon as they found the horse in front of the sage's ashram, they mistook the sage unhesitatingly for the thief, and began to wage war with him. The innocent sage, aroused by their thoughtless actions, cursed them all and burned their ashes.

Long after this incident there arose, in the same family, another illustrious king, Bhagiratha, eager to perform the rites levied by the scriptures, to alleviate the fate of his ancestors. He consulted rishis who advised him to invoke mother Ganges. She alone could wash off the powerful curse of rishi Kapila and fulfill his desire. Bhagiratha did severe *tapas*. Pleased with his penance, mother Ganges appeared before him and directed him to one who could check her flow, as otherwise the whole earth would be submerged in her waters.

For a hundred more years Bhagiratha did rigorous penance. Pleased with his devotee, Lord Shiva readily accepted to stop the flow of Gangaji through his matted locks. "With surge, fury, and foam, the Ganges began to descend from the celestial regions. Flashes of lightning, thunder from clouds, and the uncontrollable flow seemed as if a deluge were about to devour the whole world. But Lord Shiva coolly received her in his matted locks and let her drip over him. This is (celebrated on) the Ganga Saptami day."[5]

There is again the story of the Ganges coming through Rishi Jahnu's ears. Taking her course into the interior of the Himalayas, Ganges was about to wash away Rishi Jahnu's ashram. But the sage, more powerful than she, merely sipped her waters! Bhagiratha, disappointed, did severe penance again to please Rishi Jahnu. At the last, the sage let the Ganges out of his ears. Flowing out smoothly, lovingly, she uplifted all the sixty thousand princes to the highest abode of eternal bliss. This event is celebrated as the Ganga Dussera — the tenth day of the bright half of Jeth. A big *mela* (fair) is held at Haridwar from this day to the fifteenth of Jeth; it is attended by many from the Punjab, Uttar Pradesh, and other parts of the country.

Another big *mela* — the Kartika *mela* — is held each year at Garmukhteswar in Meerut district. This place marks the site, where according to the Mahabharata Santanu, the king of Hastinapur, met the goddess Ganga in human form and made her his life's mate.

Conclusion

"In this way, O Rama, the story of the descent of the Ganga has been narrated to you at length by me," says Brahma, the overlord of gods in the Ramayana (Balakanda Canto XLIV). "Attain blessedness as a reward for listening to it. May prosperity attend you." Then he tells him the glory of hearing and reading Ganga's descent on earth. The departed forebears of the man who narrates the story which fetches wealth and renown is conducive to longevity and ensures the birth of a male issue, and also residence in heaven. He who listens to this blessed story of the descent of the Ganga. . . bids fair to attain all his desired objects. All his sins totally disappear and the span of his life as well as his fame extends (21-23).

It is no wonder, then, that even today, thousands of years after these myths were written, they are devoutly believed in. So many Hindus long to bathe in, drink of and be finally put into the Gangaji. It is their cherished hope and firm belief that as she springs from the feet of God, or His heart, so she will unceasingly flow back — carrying also whoever surrenders himself to her, on her bosom, until she reaches the source that is also the goal.

For this reason, too, in the *arati* to the Gangaji, it is written:

Sharan pade jo teri, so nar tar jata
(He who takes refuge in you, reaches the shore)

and

Ek hi bar jo teri sharanagati ata
Yamki tras mitakar, paramgati pata
Om jaya Gange mata!
(Even he who takes refuge in you but just once overcomes the troubles of death *Yama* and reaches the further shore, Hail, Mother Ganges!)

APPENDIX III

Water in *Sandhya Vandanam*

Water plays a big role in *Sandhya-vandanam*, performed at morning, noon, and evening, when light give place to darkness or darkness to light, or when the sun is at its height, the devotee praises God. I have chosen it as a sample of a ritual commonly performed and which shows how it is linked with water.

Sandhya-vandanam begins with the *achamanam* — sipping of water. It is believed that sipping it with the three mantras: *Achyataya namah, Anantaya namah, Govindaya namah* will remove all ills of body and mind. This is called *Namatrayividya* or the worship with the three names, which it is believed, will cure all diseases. The *achamanam* is performed facing the east or north. With the thumb and forefinger bent, the other three fingers make a small space in the hand to hold water, which after being poured a little, is sipped thrice while the names are uttered. The *pavitra* (or sacred ring), if worn on the second finger, should be removed at the time of the *achamanam*. Then follows the touching of the various senses or levels of the body with the washed fingers — uttering twelve names of the Lord.[1] Thus all parts of the body are protected by the Lord — through the power of His name and are dedicated to His service.

After invoking Ganapati to ward off all hindrances, doing *Pranayam* (controlled breathing while reciting the mantra *Om bhuh, Om Buvah, Om Suvah, Om Hahah*, etc. and saying the *Sankalpah*: "I worship the *ndhya* goddess of the morning to be worthy of the grace of the Supreme

Lord by the destruction of all past), the *Marjanam* purification is performed. With the second finger of the right hand, the letter *Om* is written on water, uttering *"Sri Kesavaya namah"*; then with the same finger, the center of the brow is touched.

The water is sprinkled on the head with the second finger while seven mantras are recited. With the eighth, the feet are touched, with the ninth, water is again sprinkled on the head, and while repeating *"Om Bhurbhuvasvaha"*, a circuit over the head is made.

The *Marjana mantra* is a most beautiful prayer:

Om prostration is made Sri Kesava. You water goddesses are the causes of conferring highest happiness. Even such as you. Give us nourishment for the eye of knowledge that is so great and beautiful. The Bliss most auspicious that is in you, give unto us — like a loving mother. You are love personified and the seat of that Bliss. We pray you with great earnestness to give us that Bliss. Make us pure by knowledge and be reborn, as it were, resplendently.[2]

It is interesting to note that water is used as a sacrament or sacramental; a means of obtaining God's highest grace — supreme Bliss which comes through purity attained by knowledge. It is not merely the outer washings that make us truly pure, but "the eye of knowledge" — *chakshase*. The waters are called "loving mothers" [*Ushtih matarah Iva*]: "shining with love" [*jinvatha*], who can give, to those who ask "with great eagerness" [*aram*] that bliss [*tasma*], establishing that bliss [*vasya kshayaya*] until the person is "reborn" — "give us rebirth" [*janavatha*]. This reminds us again of the words of the Lord Jesus: "Unless you are born again of water and the Spirit, you cannot enter the Kingdom of Heaven" (Jn. 3:5). The Spirit is wisdom and knowledge, who gives us that *divya chakkshu* spoken of in the Gita, without which Krishna says Arjun could not see his divine form *roopam aishvaram* (B. Gita XI.3).

After this follows the *Pratah Prashanam*, which is a prayer for forgiveness of sin, especially those born of anger, and for any evils done in the night by any part of the body, so that freed from sin the person may offer oblations to the Supreme light (the Sun) and be worthy of *moksha* (liberation).[3] During its recitation, water is taken in the right hand, in the full hollow of the palm, and drunk. It is as though water being drunk would purify one's inner being, just as bathing with it is expected to purify one's outer self — the body.

At the mid-day *Sandhya* (madhyanhe) the same gesture is accompanied by the prayer: "May the goddess of water purify the earth. May that purified earth purify me and the teachers of Vedas. May the ever purified Vedas purify me. . . I offer myself to be consumed at the blaze of the Supreme Being.'

For the evening *Sandhya*, as water is sipped, one recites: "May the Lord of Fire, God of anger, protect me from all the sins committed by anger — may my sins of the day committed by the mind, by word, the two hands, feet, stomach and the sexual organ be removed by the deity of the day. Thus purified, I offer myself as an oblation to the resplendent Supreme Light, the cause of moksha."

It is significant how anger is mentioned again. *Ahimsa*, it will be recalled, is the first of the *yama* in Patanjali Maharishi's "Yoga Sutras." So it is no wonder any kind of violence needs to be forgiven. Also the sense of sin and a felt need for purification are obvious; consciousness, too, that one oould have sinned through various parts of one's being and body.

This part of the *Sandhya Vandanam* ends with a fine prayer: May the Lord, the Support, the Ruler and the Measurer of all the worlds, the Victorious, the Seat of all knowledge, who has taken the form of *hayagriva*, the swift Supreme Lord, whom I salute, make our senses do good. May our lives be without any hindrance.

The *Arghya-pradanam* begins with the *Gayatri Mantra*. *Tad Saviturvarenyam*. . . during which before sunrise, filling both hands with water, one pours it three times to the East. At noon, facing north one pours it twice, at evening before sunset, in a sitting posture. The thumb should be apart when offering the *arghya*.[4]

In *Praysaschittarghuam*, preceded by *Pranayama*, water is poured, uttering *Om bhur-bhuva-svah*. Then one "circumambulates the head" with water. In the *Aikyanusandhanam* one recites the mantra: *Asaradityo [asare-aditya] Brahma. Brahmaivasmi*. (This sun is Braahma. I, too, am verily brahman.) Before doing *achamanam* with two hands, one touches the breast, closes the eyes, and deeply meditates on the truth that the *Jeevatman* and *Paramatman* are one.

Deva-Tarpanam is offered facing the East in the morning and at noon, facing the north in the evening; pouring water but not as a current. *Tarpayami* at the end of each invocation means "I propitiate."[5]

From Keshava up to Damodar, the twelve names of Vishnu, the

deities of the twelve months are invoked.[6]Then with the *achamanam* the first part of *Sandhya-Vandaanam* is over.

The second part of *Sandhya-Vandanam* begins with the *Japa Sankalpa*. Through the various prayers to the sun that follow water is not mentioned till the last invocation of *Madhyan*. "May the fulfiller of desired results, all-knowing, shining everywhere, rising from the midst of the water, may that sun god purify me and all my mind."

The all-knowing, shining one rises from the waters. *Japarambha* saying I shall do the "Gayatri — Mahamantra Japa," one should sit with a water vessel in front, eyes half shut, seeing nothing external facing the east in the morning, the north at noon and the west in the evening.

Then follows the *Pranava* (Om) and the *Pranayama*, when the *rishi* is named, the head is touched with the right hand; when naming the *chandas*, the mouth; when naming the *devtas*, the breast is touched.

One *pranayam* needs the *japam* of the mantra thrice, at least three *pranayam* must be done. Those not able to do *puraka, kumbhak, rechaka* (inhalation, holding the breath, exhalation), should repeat the mantra ten times.

Then follows the *Gayatri-arakanam*. Reciting this mantra, the *Gayatri Devi* is thought of an manifesting herself in the lotus of the heart. With the sign of invocation, the hands are turned inwards in front of the heart of the *Gayatri Nyasah* — the meaning is: Of the *Savitri mantra* (i.e., Gayatri), *Viswamitra* is the *Rishi*, the *Gayatri* is the meter, and the Sun is the deity.

The *Gayatri japa* — "We meditate on the Lord's most excellent light" — must be done standing facing the east morning and noon; and sitting facing the west in the evening. It should be repeated 108 times or 54, or at least 28 times, and touching the lines on the fingers. A *rudraksha* or *tulsi mala* (rosary) may be used for the *japa*.

Gayatri upasthanam is the prayer to that deity, said after the *japam*, to go to her own place — "on the top of Mount Meru, the excellent peak which is your abode *uttama shikhara*, please go." This is preceded by *pranayama*.

The *Surya upasthanam* is said with folded hands, standing, facing the East. It is the worship of *Paramatma* in the solar orb. The sun is the all-knowing, guiding, friend of the universe, protecting all from disease.

Madhyanhe — Midday *Sandhya*. One prays:

The Sun god who sees *satyene*, by the light of the self, and by the light of the eyes, gods and mortals, engaging them in their respective works, goes round in the golden chariot and travels with a particular eye on the world.

May we attain the excellent light of the soul, we who have seen the sun (god) who has the excellent light and rises to swallow darkness and is the protector of even the gods.

Water, which has not been mentioned at all from the second part of the *Sandhya Vandanam* comes again in the last prayer of *Madhyanhe*, right at the end of *Sandhya Vandanam* in the last *namaskar*: Just as the water fallen from the sky goes to the ocean, so salutation to any god who reaches *Keshava*. *Om Namah* after the *Samarpanam* — the final offering *Kayena vacha*, the whole *Sandhyaa Vandanam* once again ends with *achamanam*, sipping of water: Whatever I have done by my body, speech, mind, the senses or by my character (or my nature) I dedicate to *Narayana*, the Supreme God (Son of Man).

NOTES

Introduction

1. Bruce Vawter, "Johannine Theology," *Jerome Bible Commentary II*, 80 (Bangalore: T.P.I.), p. 829.

2. Cf. Vandana, "Indian Theologizing and the Role of Experience," paper written for an all-India Seminar on "Theologizing on India" (Poona: NVSC), October, 1978. In *Jeevadhara*, a journal of Christian interpretation, September to October, 1979. Vol. IX, No. 53. (Kerala: Theology Center).

3. Cf. *Bible Bhashyam*, an Indian biblical quarterly; issue entitled "Dhvani: As a Method of Interpretation" by F.X. D'sa S.J. (Kittayam, Kerala: St. Thomas Ap. Seminary).

4. Cf. Christopher Duraisingh and Cecil Hargreaves, eds., *India's Search for Reality and the Relevance of the Gospel of St. John*. Papers from a conference held in Christ Prem Seva Ashram, Pune, February, 1974 (Delhi: ISPCK).

5. Cf. C. Duraisingh, "The Gospel of John and the World of India Today" in *India's Search for Reality and the Relevance of the Gospel of John*.

6. Cf. C. Duraisingh, p. 45.

7. From the unreal lead me to the Real
   From darkness lead me to Light
   From death lead me to Immortality.
   Brihad. Up. 1.3.38

8. Bruce Vawter, "Johannine Theology."

9. C.H. Dodd, *The Interpretation of the Fourth Gospel* (Cambridge, 1953), p. 6.

10. The river Ganges or "Mother Ganga" — flowing from the North Indian Himalayan ranges — the highest mountains of the world — is very sacred to the Hindus.

11. St. Ignatius of Antioch: "I hear within me as from a spring of living water the murmur: 'Come to the Father.' "

Chapter One

1. Cf. *Jerome Bible Commentary II*, p. 426.
2. Cf. St. Proclus, "Oration 7" in *Sancta Theophanja* (1-3, 65, 758-759), quoted in *Text for the Office of Readings* Vol 1 (Bangalore: NBCLC), p. 221-222.
3. Ibid.
4. Cf. *Text for the Office of Readings*.
5. Cf. 1 Cor. 6:11; Eph. 5:26; Heb. 10:22; Acts 22:16. Cf. also section of the Ganges, its purificatory powers, "Ganga-*Snan*" as also the commentary on "Waters of Rebirth" on John 3 — Nicodemus — for a more detailed study of this point.
6. John Marsh, "St. John" in *Pelican New Testament Commentaries*, p. 117.
7. C.H. Dodd, *The Founder of Christianity* (London: Collins, 1971), pp. 122-123.
8. Not mentioned in John 1 but cf. Matt. 3:17; Mk. 1:11; Lk. 3:22. The prophets of the Old Testament had heard God addressing Israel in those words. Cf. Exod. 4:22; Ps. 2:7; Is. 42:1, etc.
9. Swami Abhishiktananda, *The Further Shore* (Delhi: ISPCK, 1975). This entire chapter on *Sannyasa-Diksa*, which I quote from below, is worth reading. "The new *Sannyasi* then unties all the clothes he may be wearing and lets them float away in the stream. Then the Guru calls him back to the bank and receives him in his arms" (one might say like the Father embracing the Son, in whom he is well pleased) "dripping with water and naked as he was when he came forth from his mother's womb. He then covers him with the fire color cloth of *Sannyasi*, the flame-color of the *Purusha*, of the golden Hamsa (Brihad Up. 4.3.11). One is reminded of the flame of the Spirit, the Atman, the Self of whom he is now aware, in whom all has been burned up; he is a new man or rather he is the unique man, the unique *Purusha*, the unique spirit, whom no garment can ever again clothe, other than the garment of fire, which consumes all other garments superimposed on the essential nudity of the original *Purush*, the non-dual Spirit" (p. 55).
10. J. Dupuis, *Jesus Christ and His Spirit* (Kurseong: St. Mary's College), p. 189 f.
11. Cf. J. Dupuis, *Jesus Christ and His Spirit* (Bangalore: T.P.I., 1977); cf. pp. 239, 242-243.
12. Ibid.
13. Swami Abhishiktananda, *Saccidananda* (Delhi: ISPCK, 1974), p. 95.
14. Sebastian Moore, *God Is A New Language* (London: Darton, Longman & Todd, 1970), p. 163.
15. I have risen beyond all desires, desire for progeny, desire for riches, desire for any *loka* whatever [cf. Brihad up. 3.5]; not so much as a decision for the future but what is already in the depth of his heart.
16. Abhishiktananda, *The Further Shore*, p. 52.

Chapter Two

1. Cf. Bhagavad Gita 2.54 f.
2. *Jerome Bible Commentary*, p. 424.
3. The sequence can be seen in John 1:29; 1:35; 1:39-42, 43 -four days.
4. Jn. 2:11; 4:54; 6:14; 9:16; 12:18; also dealing with water. Jn. 5:2-9; 6:16-21 describe them in detail but do not call them "signs," though they doubtless are. Cf. Bruce Vawter, "Johannine Theology," p. 833.
5. Ibid.
6. Cf. the Woman of the Apocalypse 12, who is also the Mother of Christ and of the new Israel, where the vision of John is again by the imagery of Genesis.
7. T.T. Feeney, "Waters of Salvation" in *Bible Today*, March 1965, pp. 1097-1102.
8. Joseph Ratzinger, *Introduction to Christianity* (London: Search Press, 1971), p. 197.
9. Cf. the use of the figure of an abundance of wine in Amos 9:13 f.; Hos. 14:7; Jer. 31:12; Enoch 10:19; Bar. 29:5 (Brown RE).

10. C.K. Barrett, however, says: "It remains quite uncertain whether any allusion to the Eucharist is intended." "The Gospel According to John," introduction and commentary (London: SPCK, 1979), p. 189.

11. Ratzinger, p. 197-198.

12. Cf. Leon Dufour, "Water" in *Dictionary of Biblical Theology*, (Bangalore: Theological Publications of India), p. 646.

13. Dufour, p. 646.

14. C.K. Barrett, *The Gospel According to St. John* (London: SPCK), pp. 188 f.

15. Ibid.

16. Rig Ved X.34.1; IX.98.9.

17. Rig Ved 88.24-25.

18. Cf. Motilal Pandit, *Vedic Hinduism* (Allahabad: St. Paul's), p. 76.

19. Svetasvatara Upanishad 4.15, 17.

20. Burtmann, *The Gospel of John*, quoted by C.K. Barrett.

21. *Jerome Bible Commentary II*, p. 428.

Chapter Three

1. "From darkness lead me to light (Brihad Up. 1.3.28).

2. Cf. Chapter 1 of *Waters of Awakening*.

3. Cf. *Jerome Bible Commentary*, p. 429-430.

4. C.C. Martindaale, *Princes of His People* (London: Burns Oates and Washborne, 1926), p. 41-42.

5. Cf. Leon Dufour, p. 646 f.

6. Joseph Ratzinger, *Introduction to Christianity*, p. 258.

7. Mascaro's translation of the Upanishads, *The Supreme Teaching* (Penguin Books, 1970), pp. 140-141.

8. Cf. *Sacramentum Mundi I, An Encyclopedia of Theology* Bangalore: T.P.I., 1975), p. 142.

9. Cf. Abhishiktananda, *The Further Shore*, p. 95.

10. Murray Bodo, *Francis: The Journey and the Dream* (Cincinnati: St. Anthony Messenger Press), p. 9 f.

11. Abhishiktananda, *The Further Shore*, p. 2.

12. Ibid, p. 56. Cf. Brihad Up. 4.4.23; Chando g. Up 8 end.

13. Translation of Barclay of the first Beatitude.

14. Abhishiktananda, *The Further Shore*, p. 109.

15. *Sacramentum Mundi I*, p. 144.

16. M.E. Boismard in *Dictionary of Biblical Theology*, p. 647.

17. Cf. *Sacramentum Mundi I*, p. 139-142.

18. Fergus Kerr, *Experience and Theologizing* (New Blackfriars, September, 1965), p. 171.

19. Cf. Abhishiktananda, *Saccidananda* (London: ISPCK), p. 95.

20. C.H. Dodd quoted by Marsh, p. 192.

21. John Marsh, "St. John" in *Pelican New Testament Commentary*, p. 188.

22. A Monk, "The Hermitage Within" in *Spirituality of the Desert* (London: Darton, Longman and Todd, 1977), p. 132.

Chapter Four

1. *Jerome Biblical Commentary II*, p. 431.

2. Cf. Gen. 26:14-22; Exod. 15:22-27, etc. It is significant and meaningful then, that in a painting

of the Samaritan woman by the Indian Christian artist Jyoti Sahi, Christ is seated in Padmasan (cross-legged position) on a rock, into which his whole figure merges, so that one may see Christ himself as the rock and his cupped hands held near the cave of the heart to pour out on to the woman the living streams.

3. Philippe Reymond, *L'Eau, sa vie et sa signification dans L'Ancien Testament* (Leiden: E.J. Brill, 1958), p. 200 f.

4. John Marsh, "St. John," pp. 209-210.

5. Dr. Daube, "Journal of Biblical Literature" (LXIX 1950), pp. 137-147; quoted by Marsh, p. 210.

6. Cf. Mark 7:1 f.; Lk. 11:37 f.

7. Jerusalem Bible Note on Jn. 2:20.

8. *Jerome Biblical Commentary II*, p. 431.

9. C.K. Barrett, *The Gospel According to John.*

10. Cf. Marsh, p. 214.

11. Cf. *Jerome Biblical Commentary II*, p. 432.

12. The Jewish expectation of a Messiah-Prophet — a second Moses — was based on this text. St. John's Gospel emphasizes parallels between Jesus and Moses. (Cf. Jn. 1:17 f.; 3:14, etc.)

13. *Jerome Biblical Commentary II*, p. 432.

14. Cf. Jn. 6:35; 8:12; 10:7; 10:11; 11:25; 14:6; 15:1.

15. MacNicol, *Psalms of the Maratha Saints*, p. 79.

16. Jyoti Sahi, *Meditations on Symbols of St. John's Gospel* (Pune: Art India, 1978). This is a beautiful booklet really meant to help interiorization of our own spiritual resources challenging Christians of India to "express the faith through the media of their own cultural heritage."

17. Abhishiktananda, *The Further Shore*, p. 8.

Chapter Five

1. *Jerome Biblical Commentary II*, p. 433.

2. Ibid.

3. Cf. ibid., pp. 433-434.

4. Cf. Raimundo Panikkar, *The Vedic Experience* (London: Darton, Longman and Todd, 1977), p. 116 f.

5. Cf. Arthur A. MacDonell, *A Vedic Reader for Students* (O.U.P.), pp. 67-68.

6. John Marsh, "St. John."

7. *Jerome Biblical Commentary II*, p. 434.

8. Abhishitananda, *Hindu-Christian Meeting Point* (Bangalore: CISRS, 1969), pp. 83-84. "The being of man is wholly gift, wholly grace, wholly love... I exist only at the heart of a gift."

9. John Marsh, p. 274.

10. Ibid.

11. Abhishiktananda, *The Further Shore*, pp. 61-62.

12. Ibid., pp. 61-63.

13. Cf. Jn. 1:45; 2:22; 5:39, 46; 12:16, 41; 19:28; 20:9.

14. Abhishiktananda, *The Further Shore*, p. 62.

Chapter Six

1. *Jerome Biblical Commentary II*, p. 435.

2. Padovano, quoted by Louis Bouyer, *Fourth Gospel*, (Westminster, Md.: Newman Press, 1964), on John 4.

3. Dr. Bernard I.C.C., p. 185 f. quoted in John Marsh.

4. J.N.M. Wijngaards, *Background to the Gospel* (Bangalore: T.P.I., 1974), p. 70.
5. *Jerome Biblical Commentary II*, p. 436.
6. Leon Dufour, *Dictionary of Biblical Theology*, p. 645.
7. Arthur Osborne, *The Call Divine* (1953). Cf. Jayanti Number, *The Mountain Path* (Tiruvannamalai: Ramana Ashram).
8. *Jerome Biblical Commentary II*, p. 436.
9. *The Cloud of Unknowing* (Penguin Books), pp. 59-60.
10. Ramana Maharishi, *The Mountain Path* (Jan. 1980, Vol. 17, No. 1, p. 3. Cf. Augustine: "Go not outside; return into yourself. The Truth dwells in the inner man (De Vera Religione 1.39). And Meister Eckhart: (In the inner man) "dwells God, the Truth, who cannot be reached by those who seek Him in externals, God whose natureit is to be always and only within and in the most inward place" (in Johannem).
11. Cf. St. Teresa of Avila, "Seventh Mansion" of *The Interior Castle*.
12. Abhishiktananda, *Saccidananda* (Bangalore: ISPCK), pp. 63-64.
13. *Jerome Biblical Commentary II*, p. 436, 438.
14. Cf. Katha Up. 4.1. "The Creator made the senses outward going; they go to the world of matter outside, not to the Spirit within. But a sage who sought immortality looked within himself and found the Self Existent One."
15. Al-Hallaj: Muqatt a'at. 35,10 quoted in Abhishiktananda, *Saccidananda*, p. 61.
16. Cf. Rangarajan, "The Self Beyond the Ego — Ramana Maharishi" in *Illustrated Weekly*, Feb. 17, 1980, p. 17 f.

Chapter Seven

1. Pierre Grelot on John 7:38, "Eau de rocher ou source du temple," *Revue Biblique* (1963), p. 43 f.
2. *Hiranyagarbha* is the Golden Germ, the source of golden light, the seed of all creation. Rig Ved X.82.5-6 tells us of the cosmic egg conceived as a germ by the primeval waters.
3. Cf. John Marsh, pp. 340-341.
4. Juan Mascaro, "Introduction" in *The Upanishads* (Penguin), p. 12.
5. John Marsh, p. 341.
6. *Jerome Biblical Commentary II*, p. 440.
7. John Marsh, pp. 341-342.
8. Fergus Kerr, *Experience and Theologizing* (New Blackfriars, Sept., 1965), p. 170.
9. Ibid., p. 190.
10. Ibid., p. 343.
11. Lucius Nereparampil, "Holy Spirit as Living Water" in *Bible Bhashyam* (Badvarthoor Kottayam, June 1976), p. 146, 149.
12. Cf. Abhishiktananda, *Hindu-Christian Meeting Point*, p. 80.
13. Cf. *Jerome Biblical Commentary II*, p. 441.

Chapter Eight

1. In India it is often considered crude to speak of someone's death bluntly as "he died." One says, "he left his body" (for his spirit is immortal and has not ceased to be) or "he passed on" (to another world) or "he passed away." The Gospels being Oriental too, speak in a similar vein. Cf. Jn. 13.1 "to pass from this world to the Father."
2. Jerusalem Bible Note on John 13:1.

3. Schillebeecks, *Christ, the Sacrament of Encounter with God* (London: Sheed and Ward, 1971), p. 31.

4. John Marsh, p. 483.

5. *Jerome Biblical Commentary II*, p. 451.

6. Cf. Jerusalem Bible Notes on Phil. 2:5-8.

7. Since Gahdhiji named the untouchable outcastes "Harijanas" (God's people), on his birthday the inmates of this particular Ashram go along with their Lord — to wash, feed, and fete the Harijans in this town.

8. Philippe Reymond, *L'Eau, sa vie*, p. 152.

9. John Marsh, p. 485.

10. Jerusalem Bible Note on v. 8.

11. John Marsh, p. 485.

12. Cf. *The Mountain Path*, p. 17.

13. John Marsh, p. 487.

14. *Jerome Biblical Commentary II*, p. 451.

15. Swami Sivananda, *The Way to Peace* (Durban: Divine Life Society of South Africa), p. 31.

16. C.C. Martindale, *The Household of God — St. John the Evangelist* (London: Burns Oates and Washborne, 1920), p. 94.

17. Jyoti Sahi, *Meditations on the Way of the Cross* (Pune: Marga Prakashan Snehsadan, 1980), p. 4.

Chapter Nine

1. T. Feeney, "Waters of Salvation" in *Bible Today*, March 1965, pp. 1097-1102.

2. *Jerome Biblical Commentary II*, p. 462.

3. Raymond Brown, *New Testament Reading Guide*, p. 91.

4. J. Dupuis, *Jesus Christ, Saviour and God* (Kurseong: St. Mary's College, unpublished notes), pp. 282-293.

5. A.F. Sava; cf. *Jerome Biblical Commentary II*, p. 462.

6. John Marsh, p. 621.

7. Ibid.

8. T. Feeney, pp. 1097-1102.

9. Cf. Ambrose, P.L., 15, 1585; St. Thomas, *Summa*, 3.62.5; Pius XII *Mystici Corporis* 28.

10. *Jerome Biblical Commentary II*, p. 468.

11. Cf. Jerusalem Bible Note on "Water and Blood," p. 189.

12. John Marsh, pp. 622-623.

13. Jyoti Sahi, *Meditation On the Way of the Cross*, p. 26.

14. Thising, *Per Christum in Deum*, quoted in Dupuis, S.J., *Jesus Christ Saviour and Lord*, p. 289.

15. J. Ratzinger, *Introduction to Christianity*, pp. 179-180.

16. J. Ratzinger, p. 181.

17. Ibid., p. 179.

18. Savujya, from *Yuj*, the same root from which comes *Yoga*, which means "yoking," "oneing"; cf. Latin *Jugum*.

19. J. Dupuis, pp. 291-300.

20. Jeanne de Charry, *History of the Constitutions of the Society of the Sacred Heart*, 1975; cf. chapter 1 for the outline of the devotion here given.

21. Bonaventure, *De Vita Mystica*; cf. Third Nocturne, Matins — Office of the Church for the Feast of the Sacred Heart.

22. Cf. Abhishiktananda, *Hindu-Christian Meeting Point*, p. 78.

23. Marie-Terese de Lescure — Superior General of the Society of the Sacred Heart, in her unpublished letters.

24. Dionysius, "Mystical Teaching" in *The Cloud of Unknowing and Other Works* (Penguin Books, 1978), p. 206.

Chapter Ten

1. John Marsh, pp. 659-660.
2. *Jerome Biblical Commentary II*, p. 464.
3. John Marsh, p. 661.
4. Bhagwan Shree Rajneesh, *Meditation, the Art of Inner Ecstasy* (Rajneesh Foundation, 1976), p. xiv.
5. Jerome's interpretation is interesting: ancient zoologists calculated the species of fish at precisely 153 — symbolizing that the disciples would "fish" all kinds of men.
6. John Marsh, p. 671. Probably no distinction is intended between "lambs" and "sheep." Cf. Acts 20:28; 1 Pet. 2:25; 5:2-4.
7. W. Grundman quoted in Franz Mussner, *The Historical Jesus in the Gospel of St. John* (London: Burns and Oates, 1966), p. 56.

Appendix I

1. A.A. MacDonell, *A Vedic Reader for Students* (OUP, 1976), p. 116.
2. Raimundo Panikkar, *The Vedic Experience*, p. 116.
3. Ibid., p. 601.
4. A.A. MacDonell, pp. 67-68.
5. Cf. Gen. 1:2 and Acts 2:3.
6. A.A. MacDonnell, p. 67.
7. R. Panikkar, p. 117.
8. Ibid., p. 116.
9. Cf. P.V. Kane, *History of Dharmashastra* Vol. IV (Bhandarkar Research Institute), p. 321.
10. See Appendix II on the Ganga.
11. Cf. "Waters in the Bible."
12. R. Panikkar, p. 116.
13. Cf. Philippe Reymond, *L'Eau, Sa vie*, p 184.

Appendix II

1. Swami Sivananda, *Light Divine* (Durban: Divine Life Society fo South Africa), p. 35.
2. Ibid., p. 35 f.
3. Swami Sivananda, *Mother Ganges* (Rishikesh: Divine Life Society, 1962), pp. 5-6.
4. P.V. Kane, *History of Dharma Shastra*, Vol. IV (Poona: Bhanderkar Oriental Institute, 1953), pp. 826-827.
5. Swami Sivananda, *Mother Ganges*, p. 12.

Appendix III

1. Keshava-Narayana — the thumb touching right and left cheeks, regarded as seats of fire.
Madhava Govinda — the second finger touching the eyes, regarded as seats of the Sun.
Vishnu-Madhusoodhana — the forefinger touching the nose, seat of Vayu or wind.
Tritikarma-Vamana — little finger touching the ears, seat of India.·
Shridhara-Hrishikesha — middle finger touching the shoulders, seat of Prajapati.
Padmanabha-Damordara — the inner part of hand touching the heart and top of the head, both seats of Parmatma.

2. Waters verily cause bliss. . . for the eye of knowledge. That most auspicious bliss, for that make us worthy, like living mothers, for that we go in with great eagerness. For establishing that bliss you shine with love. Waters, make us pure by knowledge; give us rebirth.

3. The sun we anger and the god of anger, all actions done by anger from sins protect (me) at night, from sins done by the mind, speech, hands, by the feet, stomach, sex organs. May the night deity remove them, that all sin in me being removed, I may receive *moksha*.

4. No explanation or reason is given for this; cf. P. Seshadri, *Sandhyavandanam* (Bharatiya Vidya Bhavan, Bombay), p. 16.

5. Thus: Adityam tarpayami — I propitiate the Sun. Soman tarpayami — I propitiate the Moon. Angarakam — Mars. Budham — Mercury. Brihaspatim — Jupiter. Shukram — Venus. Shanaischaran — Saturn. Rahum — Rahu. Ketum — Ketu.

6. See Note 1 for these twelve names.

GLOSSARY OF TERMS

Abba. Aramaic for "Father."
Advaita. Nonduality.
Agape. Greek for "love."
Agni. Fire.
Aham. I.
Ahamkar. The conception of onself as an individual, self-conceit.
Aham asmi. I am.
Aham Brahmasmi. I am Brahman.
Amrtam. Life; food of the gods, of immortality.
Anandam. Bliss, joy.
Anathema. Latin word for "to be considered as nothing."
Antar-yami. Indwelling controller.
Anubhava. Experience.
Apas. Water.
Apam napat. Son of waters.
Arati. A symbolic gesture of worship done with flowers, incense, etc.
Asat. Unreality.
Ashrama. Abode of asceticism.
Ashrama. Stage of life.
Asti. He is.
Atman. "Self."
Avatar. Incarnation.
Avidya. Ignorance.

Bhajans. Hymns of a repetitive type.

Bhakta. Devotee, lover of God.

Bhashya. Commentary.

Bet'esdatayin. House of the double gusher, a Semitic phrase.

Brahma muhrt. Intimacy with the Lord in meditation, made before sunrise.

Chit. Awareness, perception, thought.

Darsan. Sight, vision, coming into the presence of God; also a philosophical system.

Devas. Vedic gods; personified divine powers at work in the cosmos and in man; manifestation of the divine in itself (brahman), but never to be confused with it.

Dharana. Concentration of attention.

Dhyanv. Meditation leading to complete inner silence.

Divya chakshu. Divine sight.

Dvani. Method of interpreting the scriptures.

Ekagratha. One-pointedness.

Eschaton. A Greek word meaning "the end," particularly the end of the world, and so referring to the transcosmic realities seen symbolically as revealed at the end of time.

Evamvid. One who knows thus.

Fons vivus. Latin for "vivifying spirit."

Gangamata. Mother Ganga.

Gopis. Maids.

Guha. Cave, metaphorically used for the cave of the heart.

Guhacare. Moving in the cave.

Guhahita. Abiding in the cave.

Guhasaya. Resting in the cave.

Guru. Spiritual guide.

Guru-kripa. Blessing of guru.

Guruvar. The day of the guru.

Hiranyagarbha. Golden germ.

Ignis carita. Latin for "enkindling love"

Jeevan-djara. Living streams.

Jnan. True wisdom.

Jnani. Wise man.

Jyoti. Light.

Karma. Action, ritual, work, the result of acts done in a previous life.

Karma-yoga. Way of work.

Karma-yogi. One who follows the path of work to reach salvation.

Kenosis. Self-emptying.

Kyah. Life.

Leela. Play.

Logos. Greek word for referring to "God the Son."

Loka. World.

Loka-sangrah. Welfare of the world.

Loutran. Bath.

Madhu-vidya. Madhu, honey.

Mahavakya. The great sentences or mantras that sum up the teaching of the Upanishads.

Mananam. Thinking of the word.

Mantra. Formula of prayer.

Marga. Path.

Maun vyakhya. Silent discourse.

Moksha. Final liberation.

Mrtyoma amritam gamaya. From death lead me to life.

Mrtyu. Death *mrtyunjaya* — victory over death.

Mukti. Liberation.

Mumukshutva. Longing for liberation.

Murtis. Idols, images.

Namjap. Repetition of God's name.

Nam and roop. Name and form.

Nididhyasanam. Pondering.

Nimitta Matra. An occasion and an excuse.

Nishkama karma. Service without looking for any reward.

Obaudiro. From listening comes obedience.

Om tat sat. That which is.

Padmasan. The lotus posture.

Pad-puja. The act of worshipping the feet of the guru.

Paduka. The feet or sandals made of stone or metal which symbolize the presence of the Guru.

Panchang pranam. Prostration touching the five limbs (head, hands, and knees) on the floor.

Patita. The fallen ones.

Phileo. Greek word for "love."

Pitach tvamev. "You are our Father."

Pleroma. Fullness.

Pneuma. Greek word for "Spirit."

Poorna kubmha. Pot filled to the brim.

Prabodha. Awakening.

Prana. Breath.

Pratyahara. Withdrawal from things of sense.

Prem-jnan. Love and knowledge.

Puja. Worship.
Purusha. The primordial or the archetypal man.
Purnam adah. Fullness beyond.
Purnam idam. Fullness here.
Rabbi. Hebrew word for "teacher."
Rasa. Capacity to relish.
Rasa-jnata. One who experiences the *rasadhavani.*
Rishi. Seer.
Ruah. Aramaic word for "Spirit."
Sat. Being.
Saccidananda. Being, consciousness, bliss, the Hindu mystery nearest to the Trinity.
Sadhana. Spiritual discipline.
Sadhu. A monk.
Sahaja. Friendly.
Sakti. Force, power, energy, the active power of the Divinity manifested throughout the created universe.
Salokya. Living in the same place as God.
Samipya. Living close to God.
Samsara. The world as seen in the ceaseless flux of its cycles, passing through successive births and deaths.
Sannyasi. One who has given himself to cosmic life.
Sannyasa-diksha. Ceremony of initiation into *sannyasa.*
Sarupya. Having the same form as God; conformed to Him.
Sarva-dwar-bandh. Thorough control of and closing of the doors of the senses.
Sarvatondmukhaya. One whose face is turned everywhere, one whose face shines through any and every human face.
Sarx. Greek word for "flesh."
Sat. Truth, reality.
Satguru. Supreme Teacher.
Sayujya. Union with God.
Sentire et gustare res interne. To taste and relish the inner things.
Seva. Service.
Shastras. Sacred texts.
Siloam. The name of a pool in Jerusalem; literally it means "sent."
Soma. The beverage of god "Indra."
Scruti. Musical note.
Sthitaprajna. Steadfast wisdom.
Sunya. The Buddhist concept of nothingness.
Tadvanam. Love longing.
Tamas. Darkness.

Tanpura. Instrument which helps in the keeping of rhythm in music.
Tat. That.
Tattvam-asi. That thou art.
Tohu-tohu. A mess.
Torah. Jewish law book.
Tvameva Mata. "You are my mother."
Upanayana. Initiation ceremony.
Varuna. God of waters.
Vidya. Knowledge.
Vivek. Discrimination.
Yahweh. Word denoting God in Hebrew.
Yagna. Sacrifice.
Yama. God of death.